nihongo

situational japanese 5

by osamu mizutani
nobuko mizutani

The Japan Times

First edition: July 1990

Jacket design by Koji Detake

ISBN4-7890-0523-2

Copyright © 1990 by Osamu Mizutani and Nobuko Mizutani

All rights reserved, including the right to reproduce this book
or portions thereof in any form.

Published by The Japan Times, Ltd.
5-4, Shibaura 4-chome, Minato-ku, Tokyo 108, Japan

Printed in Japan

FOREWORD

This book is a compilation of the 74 columns appearing in *The Japan Times* from December 1988 to May 18, 1990. (The preceding 646 columns have been published as *Nihongo Notes 1-9*. *Nihongo Notes 6, 7, 8* and *9* are entitled *Situational Japanese 1, 2, 3* and *4*.)

It is a great pleasure for us to be able to publish another volume in this series, and we are very grateful for your continued interest. We hope that you will enjoy reading this volume and that it will help you to understand the Japanese language more fully and precisely.

In this volume, we have attempted to discuss, among other things, how the Japanese express themselves for such purposes as stating an opinion, thanking someone for some service, offering to do a favor, giving advice, and giving compliments. We have also tried to explain the subtle difference between two similar expressions and show how a foreigner can avoid making mistakes in using them. Throughout, we have concentrated on actual speech patterns used in daily communication.

For the convenience of the reader, we have added a list of the words and phrases discussed in the five volumes of *Nihongo Notes 6-10* as well as an index to important expressions classified according to usage.

We would like to acknowledge the help of Janet Ashby, who checked the English for these columns and offered valuable suggestions just as she did for the preceding nine volumes.

June, 1990
Osamu and Nobuko Mizutani

CONTENTS

. . . hodo used in formal speech 8

Yatsu meaning 'fellow, stuff' 10

Nantoka used to mean 'one can manage' 12

Expressing gratitude for service 14

Addressing someone by name 16

Expressions used for admiration................... 18

Chikaku (almost) and *chotto* (a little more than).. 20

Hodo indicating degree 22

Making verbs from adjectives...................... 24

. . . atsukai meaning 'treating someone as'....... 26

Expressions meaning 'why' 28

. . . kankee meaning 'related to . . .' 30

Offering to do a favor 32

Kara and *node* (because, since) 34

Expressions meaning 'everything' 36

Expressions meaning 'Isn't it . . . ?' 38

Ureshii and *koofuku* (happy) 40

A use of *kore-wa* (this is)............................. 42

. . . ni . . . ni (A and B and C) 44

Expressions meaning 'but' 46

Ohayoo-gozaimasu (Good morning) 48

Uses of *toka* (and) 50

O added to adjectives 52

Chuu (while) and *juu* (all through) 54

Ookii and *ookina* (big) 56

Okusan and *Yoshiko-san* 58

Chuushi-suru (call off) and *chuushi-ni naru* (be called off).. 60

Gachi (be apt to, tend to) 62

. . . ni totte (for. . .) 64

4

Hazukashigariya (a shy person) 66

Gomen (Pardon) 68

Darake (filled with) 70

Kagi-ga kakatte-imasu (It's locked) 72

... *mono* used to make expressions indirect 74

Amari . . . nai (not . . . much) (1) 76

Eki-made aruku (walk as far as the station) 78

Expressions meaning 'should have' 80

... *no koto* meaning 'about . . .' 82

Dattara meaning 'if that is the case' 84

Hotondo meaning 'almost all' 86

Kiita ato-de and *kiite-kara* (after asking him) 88

Zeekin-o torareru (to have to pay texes) 90

Ya, a familiar sentence particle.................... 92

Expressions used for praise 94

Okaimono-desu-ka (Are you shopping?)........... 96

... *te-kuru* indicating the start of an action 98

... *dooshi* meaning 'keep . . . ing'.................. 100

Uses of *kekkoo* (good) 102

Kotowaru meaning 'to give previous notice' 104

Gakusee-ni suginai (He's only a student) 106

... *mo aru-shi*, ... *mo aru* (There are . . . and
...) 108

Ima hitotsu meaning 'something more is needed'.. 110

Apologies and the use of *kara* 112

The differences between *wa* and *mo* 114

Expressions meaning 'I think that . . .'........... 116

Sanji-ni (at three) and *sanji-kara* (from three) .. 118

Dareka inai-ka-to omotte . . . (wondering if there
isn't someone . . .) 120

Nanishiro used for emphasis........................ 122

Nandaka preceding the expression of feeling ... 124

Tema (one's time/labor) 126

Expressions indicating the cause of emotion .. 128

Kurushii and *tsurai* (painful) 130
. . . *dano* . . . *dano* (. . . and . . .) 132
Amari . . . *nai* (not . . . much) (2) 134
Nuances of . . . *n-da-kara* 136
. . . *eba* used for giving advice 138
Soo omoimasu (I think so) 140
. . . *te* meaning 'a person who 142
Ichido and *ikkai* (one time) 144
Yoru (draw near) 146
. . . *ni kansuru* (concerning . . .) 148
Expressions meaning 'to me, for me' 150
Gaman-suru (to be patient, to endure) 152
Kochira (this side, me) 154

General Index (Volumes 6-10) 157
Index to Words, Phrases and Sentences
    (Volumes 6-10) 167

Note Concerning Romanization

The romanization used in this book (as well as in *An Introduction to Modern Japanese*) is based on the Hepburn system with the following modifications.

1. When the same vowel occurs consecutively, the letter is repeated rather than using the "-" mark.
   ex. *Tookyoo* (instead of *Tōkyō*)
2. The sound indicated by the hiragana ん is written with "*n*" regardless of what sound follows it.
   ex. *shinbun* (instead of *shimbun*)
   ex. *shinpai* (instead of *shimpai*)

The words connected with hyphens are pronounced as one unit.
   ex. *genki-desu*
   ex. *Soo-desu-ne.*

... *hodo* used in formal speech

Mr. Lerner and Miss Yoshida had dined together and were walking leisurely along the street last Saturday evening. When they casually dropped in at a jewelry shop, Miss Yoshida pointed to a rather expensive-looking ring, asking the salesman

Kore, ikahodo-desu-ka.
これ、いかほどですか。

and the man told her the price. Mr. Lerner was interested in the word *ikahodo*. He understood from the situation that it was equivalent to *ikura* (how much), but he had never heard her use it before. When he mentioned it afterwards, she looked a little embarrassed and wondered why she had used it.

*   *   *

Hodo, which means "degree" or "extent," is usually added to other words. It is used in its original meaning in such words as *kore-hodo* (this extent), *sore-hodo/are-hodo* (that extent) and *dore-hodo* (what extent). When it is added to words indicating number or amount, it means "approximately," as in *sen-en-hodo* (about ¥1,000) and *mikka-hodo* (about three days).

When added to certain words, *hodo* makes them sound more formal. *Ika-hodo* is made up of *ika-* (how) and *hodo*; it means "how" in written language, but in conversation it means "how much." *Ika-hodo* sounds more formal and refined than *ikura*. Miss Yoshida probably used this word because the store looked exclusive and she was referring to an expensive-looking jewel.

There are several words with *hodo* which sound

formal; they are often used in public announce-
ments, by salespersons dealing with expensive
merchandise and employees at high-class hotels
and restaurants.

Nochi-hodo shachoo-ga o-ukagai-itashimasu.
のちほど
(The conductor will come by to serve you later.)

Saki-hodo okyakusama-ni denwa-ga gozaimashita.
さきほど
(There was a telephone call for you a little
while ago, ma'am.)

Toire-wa tsuuro-no naka-hodo-ni gozaimasu.
(The rest room is midway down the hall.)

Yatsu meaning 'fellow, stuff'

Miss Yoshida and Mr. Kobayashi, the youngest worker at the office, were talking at lunch yesterday. When Mr. Lerner approached them he heard Miss Yoshida saying

Ne, sore, donna yatsu?
どんな　やつ

Mr. Lerner thought she meant "What kind of fellow is he?" He was surprised because he had thought *yatsu* was used only by men. Miss Yoshida noticed his surprise and explained that they were talking about a new type of pocket calculator, not a man; she hurriedly added that she used *yatsu* only in conversation with young people.

*　　　*　　　*

The word *yatsu* usually means "a fellow," "a guy," as in

Yamada-tte ii yatsu-dayo.
(Yamada is a nice guy.)

It is used only in familiar conversation, largely by men. When *yatsu* refers to persons, it often implies emotions like contempt or affection; the particular emotion depends on the context.

Anna yatsu, nido-to aitaku nai.
あんな　やつ、二度と　会いたく　ない。
(I don't want to see such a fellow again.)

implies disgust or contempt, while saying

Kawaii yatsu-nanda, uchi-no inu.

10

(My dog is such a good dog.)

implies affection.

However, *yatsu* is sometimes used to mean "thing," or "stuff" as in

>*Kondo atarashii yatsu-ga deta-yo.*
>あたらしい　やつ
>(A new type is on sale now.)

referring to such things as cars, machines, etc. Women sometimes use it in familiar conversation in this sense, as Miss Yoshida did. In this usage *yatsu* resembles *no*, as in *atarashii-no* (a new one).

Yatsu is often used together with *ko* (this), *so* (that), *a* (that over there), and *do* (which); when combined with these words, *yatsu* changes into *itsu* as in

>*koitsu* (this fellow, this one)
>*soitsu* (that fellow, that one)
>*aitsu* (that fellow, that one)
>*doitsu* (which fellow, which one)

Nantoka used to mean 'one can manage'

Mr. Lerner and Mr. Takada were working busily yesterday afternoon. Around 5 o'clock Mr. Takada came by to ask Mr. Lerner how he was doing, and he answered

Nan-to naku owarimasu.

meaning "I will manage to finish it somehow." Mr. Takada agreed, but it appeared that Mr. Lerner's response was not quite appropriate.

*   *   *

Nan-to naku literally means "for nothing in particular" or "for no particular reason"; it can be translated as "somehow or other," but it is usually followed by an expression of emotion or supposition, as in

Nan-to naku kyoo-wa ikitaku nai.
なんと　なく　きょうは　行きたく　ない。
(Somehow I don't feel like going today.)
Nan-to naku ano-hito-wa konai yoona ki-ga suru.
(I somehow feel that he will not be coming.)

In Mr. Lerner's sentence above, he should have used *nantoka* instead. *Nantoka*, which literally means "by some means or other," is used to express effort or success with much difficulty.

Nantoka ma-ni awaseru yoo-ni doryoku-shimasu.
(I will do my best to make the deadline.)
Nantoka ma-ni atta.
なんとか　間に　合った。
(I managed to make it in time.)

Mr. Lerner could have said to explain his situation

Nantoka owaru-to omoimasu.
(I think I can manage to finish.)
Nantoka owarasemasu.
(I will try to finish it by some means or other.)

Since it implies difficulty, one sometimes uses this phrase in making a request:

Muzukashii-towa omoimasu-ga, nantoka onegai-shimasu.
(I know it will be difficult, but could you try?)

It is also used as an answer to "How is it going?":

Maa, nantoka yatte-imasu.
まあ、なんとか　やっています。
(I'm managing somehow.)

Expressing gratitude for service

Mr. Lerner and Miss Yoshida dined together at a Japanese restaurant last Saturday. As they were leaving, Miss Yoshida said to an employee there

Osewasama-deshita.
おせわさまでした。
(Thank you for your trouble.)

Mr. Lerner wondered if *Gochisoosama* ごちそうさま was also appropriate in this situation.

*　　　*　　　*

Employees at Japanese restaurants express their gratitude quite politely to their customers, while many customers just leave without saying anything at all. Customers are not expected to say anything in return; some of them just nod but other customers say *Gochisoosama* (*lit.* Thank you for your feast) or *Gochisoosama-deshita* (more polite) when leaving a restaurant.

Osewasama-deshita is often used when leaving a hotel or inn, especially when the customer has received familylike care or some special service. Miss Yoshida must have used this expression when leaving the restaurant because she had gotten special service from that employee.

Gokuroosama is often used with a delivery man or someone who has gone on an errand for you. It is not usually used at a restaurant, although you can use it in such cases as when you have asked an employee to go and buy cigarettes for you. Nowadays people have come to use this expression less often because they feel that it reflects a master-servant relationship. Instead they use *Arigatoo* or *Osewasama.*

14

Arigatoo can be used in place of such expressions as *Gochisoosama*, *Osewasama* and *Gokuroosama*. But it should be kept in mind that *Arigatoo* is used only when you do not have to be polite. When thanking an acquaintance or someone you do not know, *Arigatoo-gozaimasu* is more appropriate.

Addressing someone by name

Mr. Lerner was discussing a new project with the director of the company and several workers. When the discussions were over, Mr. Takada remarked that Mr. Lerner often added the names of the persons he was talking to, as in

Hai, wakarimashita, Katoo-san.
(I understand, Mr. Kato.)
Sore-wa muri-kamo shiremasen, Mori-shachoo.
(That might be impossible, Director Mori.)

Mr. Lerner asked him if it sounded impolite. He answered no, but that it somehow sounded strange.

* * *

In Japanese one uses another's name when one wants to attract his attention, as in

Yoshida-san, chotto kore mite-kudasai.
(Please take a look at this, Miss Yoshida.)
Takada-san, sore-wa chigau-to omoimasu-yo.
(I don't think so, Mr. Takada.)

But using someone's name does not serve to make the tone polite or familiar. In English it sounds more polite to say "I understand, Mr. Kato" than just saying "I understand." Or, it adds intimacy to use someone's first name as in "I agree with you, Mary" or "That's it, John." Japanese do not use personal names for such a purpose. Politeness or familiarity is expressed by various other devices, such as using different verbs or different verb forms.

Teachers often notice that foreigners add the instructor's name in the classroom, as in

Maeda-sensee, shitsumon-ga arimasu.
(I have a question, Mrs. Maeda.)
Shitsumon-ga arimasu, Maeda-sensee.
(I have a question, Mrs. Maeda.)

A Japanese would say, in the same situation,

Sensee, shitsumon-ga arimasu.
先生、質問が　あります。
or
Shitsumon-ga arimasu.

The teacher's name, *Maeda*, is not used because the student does not have to distinguish Mrs. Maeda from other teachers, since there is usually only one *sensee* in the classroom.

Expressions used for admiration

It was a lovely day yesterday. Miss Yoshida looked out at the sky during their coffee break and said

Maa, kireena sora. (What a beautiful sky!)

Mr. Lerner joined her, saying

Honto-ni suteki-desu-ne.

meaning "It really is beautiful."

Miss Yoshida said *suteki* sounded feminine, and the several workers there agreed. Mr. Lerner wondered if he could have said *utsukushii* (beautiful) instead.

*   *   *

Among several expressions used to admire something or someone, *kiree* is most commonly used in conversation. Mr. Lerner could have said *Honto-ni kiree-desu-ne* to agree with Miss Yoshida. The word *utsukushii* is more appropriate in written language or in formal speech.

Mr. Lerner could also have said

Subarashii-desu-ne.　すばらしいですね。

to admire the beauty of the sky. *Subarashii* is used to express one's admiration of both concrete and abstract things, as in

Subarashii e-desu-ne.
(It is a masterpiece — a wonderful painting.)
Subarashii ensoo-deshita.
(It was a marvelous performance.)

It sounds more emphatic and elated than *kiree*.

Suteki is used mostly by women, as Miss Yoshida said. It is quite often used by young women to express their admiration with warmth, as in

> *Ano-hito, suteki!* あの人、すてき！
> (How nice he is!)
> *Oyasumi-ga mikka tsuzuku-nante suteki-dawa.*
> (How nice it is to have a three-day holiday.)

Men sometimes use it, but that is limited to such cases as talking to women about something feminine. A salesman might say

> *Kore-nado, sutekida-to omoimasu.*
> (I think this is very nice.)

to promote a dress to a shopper.

Chikaku (almost) and *chotto* (a little more than)

Mr. Takada wore a new, fashionable suit to the office the other day. Miss Yoshida admired it and said it must have been expensive. Someone said

> *Juuman-chikaku shita-deshoo?*
> (It must have cost almost 100,000 yen.)

Then Mr. Takada said

> *Jitsu-wa, chotto-nanda-yo.*
> (*lit.* In fact, it is a little.)

and everybody seemed impressed, although Mr. Lerner did not understand.

*   *   *

In Mr. Takada's sentence, *juuman* was left out before *chotto*. Saying *juuman-chotto* means "a little more than 100,000"; . . . *chotto* is used to mean "a little more than" or "and a little more" when added immediately after a figure, as in

> A : *Ano-hito ikutsu-kashira.*
>   (I wonder how old he is.)
> B : *Sanjuu-chotto deshoo.*
>   三十ちよっと　でしょう。
>   (He must be a little over 30 years old.)

> *Moo jippun-chotto matta-noni, mada konai.*
> (She hasn't shown up although I have waited for a little over 10 minutes now.)

To mean "a little less than" or "nearly," . . . *chikaku* is used:

Ichiman-en-chikaku haratta-noni moo kowareta.
一万円ちかく　払つたのに　もう　こわれた。
(Although I paid nearly 10,000 yen for it, it is already broken.)
Okyaku-ga hyakunin-chikaku kimashita.
(Almost 100 customers came.)

The word *hotondo* (almost, nearly) is not commonly used with figures; it is mainly used with such expressions of amount as *ichinichi-juu* (all day long) or *ichinen-juu* (the whole year).

Hotondo ichinichi-juu nete-imashita.
ほとんど　一日じゅう　ねていました。
(I was in bed almost the whole day.)

It sounds awkward to add *hotondo* to figures as in

Hotondo ichiman-en haratta.
(I paid almost 10,000 yen.)
Hotondo hyakunin kimashita.
(Almost 100 people came.)

Hodo indicating degree

Recently Miss Yoshida said that she wanted to be excused early because she seemed to have caught a cold. When Mr. Lerner suggested that she stay home the next day, she answered

> *Iie, yasumu hodo-ja arimasen-kara.*
> (*lit.* No, it's not to the degree of being absent.)

Mr. Lerner thought he would have said *yasumanakute-mo daijoobu-desu* (I won't have to be absent), and wondered if . . . *hodo-ja nai* is a common expression.

*   *   *

The word, *hodo* is usually added to other words, and can be used in several different ways. One use is to indicate approximate amount, as in

> *Ichiman-en-hodo kashite-kuremasen-ka.*
> (Could you lend me about 10,000 yen?)
> *Mikka-hodo yasumimasu.*
> (I'll be away from work for about three days.)

In this usage, *hodo* resembles *gurai*; *gurai* can replace *hodo* in sentences like the two above, but *hodo* sounds more formal.

When *hodo* is added to nouns and pronouns, it indicates comparison:

> *Yamada-san-hodo hayaku-wa hashiremasen.*
> (I can't run as fast as Mr. Yamada.)

> A: *Senmonka-no yoo-desu-ne.*
> (You're as good as a specialist.)

22

B: *Iie, sore-hodo-ja arimasen.*
いいえ、それほどじゃ　ありません。
(No, I'm not that good.)

. . . *gurai* is also used to indicate comparison, but it is usually used in affirmative sentences, while . . .*hodo* is most often used in the negative.

Kimura-san-wa Yamada-san-gurai hayaku hashire-masu.
(Mr. Kimura can run as fast as Mr. Yamada.)

. . . *hodo* can also be used following verbs, as in Miss Yoshida's sentence above. When referring to a cold, one might say things like

Kusuri-o nomu hodo-ja arimasen.
(It's not so bad that I have to take medicine — *lit.* not to the degree of drinking medicine.)
Oisha-san-ni mite-morau hodo-ja nai-n-desu.
お医者さんに　みてもらう　ほどじゃ　ないんです。
(It's not so bad that I have to see a doctor.)

Making verbs from adjectives

After having lunch at a restaurant yesterday, Mr. Lerner and Mr. Takada suggested to Miss Yoshida that they take a walk instead of going directly back to the office. She said she would rather go back because it was very cold outside. Mr. Takada said

Sonna-ni samugaru-nowa, toshiyori-mitai-dane.
(You are like an old woman, not being able to take the cold. — *lit*. Minding the cold to that extent is like an old person.)

Mr. Lerner understood what that meant, but wasn't sure how to use the expression *samugaru* himself.

* * *

When . . . *garu* is added to the stem of *tai* (want to) and adjectives like *samui* and *omoshiroi*, it forms a verb meaning "to act in the way of. . . ." Namely, *ikitagaru* means "someone expresses the desire to go," and *samugaru* means "someone indicates that he feels very cold."

Minna ikitagatte-imasu. (Everybody wants to go.)
　　行きたがる
Dare-datte hoshigarimasu.
　　　　ほしがる
(Anyone would want to have it.)
Kono-goro-no kodomo-wa yoku samugaru.
　　　　　　　　　　寒がる
(Children these days often complain about the cold.)
Minna nani-o omoshirogatte-iru-n-daroo.
(I wonder what everybody is so amused by.)

24

To refer to someone else's feelings, . . . *to itte-imasu* or . . . *soo-desu* is used as in

> *Ano-hito-wa samui-to itte-imasu.*
> (He says he's cold.)
> *Ano-hito-wa samusoo-desu.*
> (He looks cold.)

instead of saying *Ano-hito-wa samui-desu.* Compared with these expressions, *samugatte-imasu* gives a more vivid impression as if you could see a picture of the person shivering with cold.

Because of this, you cannot use . . . *garu* or . . . *gatte-imasu* when referring to someone to whom you should pay respect; saying something like

> *Sensee-wa ocha-o nomitagatte-imasu.*

would sound as if the professor were thirsty and impatiently yelling with an empty teacup in his hand, which would detract from his dignity.

... *atsukai* meaning 'treating someone as'

Mr. Lerner visited the Takadas last Saturday. When he arrived, Mrs. Takada was preparing dinner in the kitchen, and asked him to help himself to tea, adding

> *Uchi-ja okyakusama-atsukai-shimasen-kara.*
> お客様あつかい
> (We won't treat you as a guest.)

Mr. Lerner wondered if one could also say *okyakusama-to shite atsukaimasen* to mean the same thing.

* * *

... *atsukai* is from the verb *atsukau* (to treat someone/something as ...); it is added to various nouns as in

> *Toshiyori-atsukai-shinaide-kudasai. Mada wakai-n-*
> 年寄りあつかい
> *desu-kara.*
> (Please do not treat me as an old person. I am still young.)
> *Moo otona-na-n-da-kara, kodomo-atsukai-shima-*
> 子供あつかい
> *sen-yo.*
> (Since you are now grown up, I won't treat you as a child.)

Okyakusama-atsukai means treating someone purely as a visitor, namely, serving him things and attending to him carefully, while not allowing him to participate in family life. *Okyakusama-atsukai-shimasen* usually is an expression of hospitality meaning "we regard you as a member of the family."

... *to shite atsukau* can also mean "to treat

26

someone as . . ." However the verb *atsukau* is often used with inanimate objects, and using this verb with a person can sound as if one regards him as an inanimate being. Instead, . . . *atsukai-suru* is commonly used to mean "to treat someone as . . ."

To give a few additional common usages including *atsukai, gaijin-atsukai* and *tomodachi-atsukai* are used as in

Moo Nihon-ni kite-kara nagai-n-desu-kara, gaijin-atsukai-shinaide-kudasai.
(Since I have lived in Japan for a long time, please do not treat me as a foreigner.)
Wakai sensee-na-node, seeto-tachi-ga tomodachi-atsukai-shite-iru.
(Since the teacher is very young, his pupils treat him like a friend.)

Expressions meaning 'why'

Yesterday morning Mr. Lerner overheard Mr. Takada scold Miss Yoshida about something, saying

Nan-datte boku-ni iwanakatta-n-da.
なんだって ぼくに 言わなかったんだ。
(Why didn't you tell me?)

Mr. Lerner understood that Mr. Takada was criticizing her for doing something without asking his opinion, and he wondered if *nan-datte* means "why" just like *naze*.

*   *   *

There are several expressions meaning "why" in Japanese. *Naze* can be used both in the written and spoken language.

Naze konna mondai-ga okita-noka, yoku kangaete-minakere-ba naranai.
(We should think carefully about why this kind of problem has occurred.)
Naze watashi-ni iwanakatta-n-desu-ka.
なぜ わたしに 言わなかったんですか。
(Why didn't you tell me?)

In daily conversation, *dooshite* (*lit.* by doing what?) is very often used to mean "why"; it sounds more conversational than *naze*. Especially when used with *desu-ka*, *dooshite-desu-ka* is preferred to *naze-desu-ka* because it sounds less demanding.

Another conversational expression meaning "why" is *nande*. This is used in familiar speech, and is also more demanding in tone than *dooshite*.

Nande konna-ni okureta-no.
(Why are you so late?)
Nande watashi-ni iwanakatta-no.
なんで わたしに 言わなかったの。
(Why didn't you tell me?)

Nan-datte, which Mr. Takada used when scolding Miss Yoshida, also sounds familiar; it is often used for criticizing or blaming someone, as in

Kare, nan-datte kotowatta-n-daroo.
(I don't understand why he refused.)

Mr. Takada used *nan-datte* in the case above because he was angry and wanted to blame Miss Yoshida. He would have sounded less critical if he had said

Dooshite boku-ni iwanakatta-n-da.
どうして ぼくに 言わなかったんだ。

. . . kankee meaning 'related to . . . '

At a party last week Mr. Lerner was introduced to a young woman, who said

> *Eega-kankee-no shigoto-o shite-imasu.*
> 映画関係の　仕事を　しています。
> (I work in the movie business.)

Mr. Lerner asked her if she was an actress; she laughed as if pleased, but said no. Later he found out that she was a hairdresser working with actresses. He wondered about the present-day usage of *. . . kankee*, for he hears the word used to mean various things.

*　　　*　　　*

The word *kankee* (relation) can be used by itself as in

> *Kore-to sore-towa kankee-ga nai.*
> (This has nothing to do with that.)
> *Ofutari-wa doo-yuu go-kankee-desu-ka.*
> (What relation do you two have to each other?)

Sometimes *kankee* is used to mean "reason" as in

> *Hiyoo-no kankee-de chotto muri-kamo shiremasen.*
> 費用の　関係で
> (It may be impossible because of the cost.)

Besides this usage, *kankee* is often added to other nouns to mean "in the field of" or "in the area of."

> *Hoodoo-kankee-no hito-ga kite-imasu.*
> 報道関係の　人

(Someone from the press is here to see you.)
Oji-wa shuppan-kankee-no shigoto-o shite-imasu.
(My uncle works in the field of publishing.)

Hoodoo-kankee can be used to indicate reporters, camera people, their driver or even those carrying the equipment. In the same way, *eega-kankee-no hito* includes various types of work even if just remotely related to producing films. Naturally people tend to use words with *kankee* when the occupations sound stylish or attractive.

The word *kankeesha* (someone related) is also used to mean . . . *kankee-no hito*;

Hoodoo-kankeesha-ga atsumatta.
(Many reporters came.)

To be polite, . . . *kankee-no kata* is used:

Hoodoo-kankee-no kata-wa kono saki-ewa hairema-sen.
(Reporters are not allowed to go beyond this point.)

Offering to do a favor

Mr. Lerner, Mr. Takada and Miss Yoshida went out for a drink together last Friday. After they had had a few glasses of beer and were leaving the restaurant, Miss Yoshida said

Kyoo-wa watashi-ni harawasete-kudasai.
(Today please let me pay.)

The two men thanked her and said she did not have to do so too often. Later, Mr. Lerner realized he still could not use . . . *asete-kudasai* himself.

* * *

When offering to do a favor or help with something, it is all right to use . . . *te-agemashoo* with friends or younger people:

Nimotsu, motte-agemashoo-ka.
(Shall I carry your luggage?)
Chotto tetsudatte-agemashoo.
(Let me help with that.)

However, this expression cannot be used with someone to whom you should speak politely. Instead, you can use *o . . . (ita) shimashoo.*

Onimotsu, omochi-shimashoo-ka.
お荷物、お持ちしましょうか。
(May I carry your luggage?)
Sukoshi otetsudai-(ita) shimashoo.
(Let me help you with that.)

Besides these two patterns, . . . *asete-kudasai* is also used to offer a favor or some help:

Nimotsu, motasete-kudasai.
荷物、持たせてください。
(Please let me carry your luggage.)
Sukoshi tetsudawasete-kudasai.
(Please let me help you with that.)

This expression sounds more eager, and it can be used both in polite and familiar speech. To be polite, you can add . . . *masen-ka* to *kudasai* or use . . . *te-itadakemasen-ka* instead of . . . *te-kudasai.*

Onimotsu, motasete-kudasaimasen-ka.
(Won't you let me carry your luggage?)
Sukoshi otetsudai-sasete-itadakemasen-ka.
(Won't you allow me to help you with that?)

In familiar speech, *-kudasai* is left out:

Nimotsu, motasete. 荷物、持たせて。
(Let me carry your things for you.)
Chotto tetsudawasete.
(Let me help you with that.)

Kara and *node* (because, since)

Miss Yoshida and Mr. Lerner were going to go out drinking after work last Friday. Toward the end of the day, something came up which Mr. Lerner found impossible to finish by 5, so he said:

Shigoto-ga dekita-kara, sukoshi matte-kudasai.
(I have something to do, so please wait a while.)

Miss Yoshida said OK, but Mr. Lerner wondered if he should have said *shigoto-ga dekita-node* instead.

*　　　*　　　*

Generally speaking *node* sounds more formal and reserved than *kara*, although in many cases they are interchangeable. In sentences like the ones below, either *kara* or *node* can be used:

Chotto matte-kudasai. Ocha-o iremasu-kara/node.
ちょっと　待ってください。お茶を　いれますから／ので。
(Please wait a moment. I'll make tea for you.)
Osoku narimashita-kara/node, kore-de shitsuree-shimasu.
(It's pretty late now. I'd like to say goodbye.)

But in direct requests, usually made to friends or young people, *kara* is more appropriate:

Samui-kara mado shimete.
(Close the window. I'm cold.)
Hayaku shiro-yo, jikan-ga nai-kara.
早く　しろよ、時間が　ないから。
(Do it quickly. I don't have much time.)

In the sentences above, *node* would sound awkward. But if you change the wording to express reserve or consideration, *node* as well as *kara* can be used:

    Chotto samui-node, mado shimete-kureru?
    (Would you close the window? I'm cold.)
    Amari jikan-ga nai-node, hayaku shite-moraitai-n-da-kedo.
    (I don't have much time. Could you do it quickly for me?)

The difference between *kara* and *node* is that *kara* sounds more direct and self-assertive. In Mr. Lerner's case, he would have sounded more reserved using *node* instead of *kara*.

Expressions meaning 'everything'

Mr. Ota, one of Mr. Lerner's colleagues, decided to quit his job and go to graduate school. Miss Yoshida arranged a farewell party for him, and helped him in various other ways. When he came to the office to say goodbye, he thanked her saying

> *Nani-kara nani-made osewa-ni narimashite. . .*
> 何から　何まで　おせわに　なりまして……
> (*lit.* From what to what, you helped me.)

Mr. Lerner understood that he meant "Thank you for everything you did for me," and was particularly interested in the phrase *nani-kara nani-made*. He wondered if he could have said *minna* instead.

* * *

There are several expressions that correspond to the English "everything" or "all"; *minna* and *zenbu* are the most basic ones.

> *Shigoto-wa minna/zenbu owarimashita.*
> (The work is all finished.)
> *Okane-o minna/zenbu tsukatte-shimatta.*
> (I spent all the money.)

The two are interchangeable in many cases. The difference is that *minna* sounds more conversational and often refers to people.

> *Minna-de yarimashita.*
> みんなで　やりました。
> (All of us did it together.)
> *Yaa, minna genki?*
> やあ、みんな　元気？
> (Hi, how are you, everybody?)

36

Nani-kara nani-made is used to emphasize the idea of "all" or "everything."

Nani-kara nani-made Yoshida-san-ga yatte-kure-mashita.
(Miss Yoshida did everything from A to Z for us.)

This expression is more appropriate than *minna* or *zenbu* when expressing gratitude because it emphasizes the kindness that the other person has extended to the speaker.

Expressions meaning
'Isn't it . . . ?'

Yesterday morning Mr. Lerner was looking through a Japanese newspaper before starting work, and found one of the cartoons very amusing. He laughed so loudly that Miss Yoshida looked at him with a curious look, so he said, while showing her the cartoon,

Kore, omoshiroku arimasen-ka.

meaning "Isn't this amusing?" She agreed but it seemed that his sentence was not quite right.

*　　　*　　　*

If Mr. Lerner had said

Kore, omoshiroi-ja arimasen-ka.

Miss Yoshida would have agreed more readily.

. . . *ku arimasen-ka* is mostly used to express the speaker's concern regarding another rather than emphasizing a judgment. For instance, saying

Oishiku arimasen-ka. (*lit.* Is it not delicious?)

to someone who has tasted something implies "I'm afraid you don't like it because it is not delicious." On the other hand . . . *ja arimasen-ka* is used as in:

A: *Kore tsukutte-mita-n-desu-kedo, amari yoku dekinakatta-n-desu.*
(I cooked this, but it didn't come out very well.)

B: (after tasting it) *Sonna koto arimasen-yo. Oishii-ja arimasen-ka.*

(On the contrary, it's very good, isn't it?)

Thus in the case of the cartoon mentioned above, . . . *ja arimasen-ka* should have been used.

　To give one more example, saying

　　Samuku arimasen-ka.
　　寒く　ありませんか。
　　(Isn't it cold?)

is usually followed by such sentences as *Mado-o shimemashoo-ka* (Shall I close the window?) or *Danboo-o tsukemashoo-ka* (Shall I turn the heat on?), while saying

　　Samui-ja arimasen-ka.
　　寒いじゃ　ありませんか。
　　(It's certainly cold, isn't it?)

is usually followed by such sentences as *Naze danboo-o tsukenai-n-desu-ka* (Why haven't you turned the heat on?) or *Mado-o shimenakya dame-desu-yo* (You should close the window).

Ureshii and *koofuku* (happy)

Miss Yoshida wanted to go to a concert by a very famous singer, but had almost given up on the idea because it was so difficult to get tickets for it. Then yesterday afternoon Mr. Mori, the director of the company, came in and gave her a ticket that he had somehow managed to obtain. She looked so happy holding the ticket in her hand that Mr. Lerner said

Yoshida-san, koofuku-soo-desu-ne.

meaning "You look so happy." Mr. Takada heard this, and said that *ureshisoo* should be used instead.

* * *

Both *ureshii* and *koofuku* mean "happy," but the usage is a little different. *Ureshii* is used to describe joy felt over a specific incident.

Ano toki-wa hontoo-ni ureshikatta.
あの 時は ほんとうに うれしかった。
(I felt really happy at that time.)
Sono shirase-o kiite minna ureshisoona kao-o shi-mashita.
(Everybody looked happy upon hearing that news.)

On the other hand, *koofuku* refers to a state which lasts for some time. You can say

Futari-no kekkon-seekatsu-wa koofuku-datta.
二人の 結婚生活は 幸福だった。
(The two lived happily together as man and wife.)

40

But you cannot use *ureshikatta* in place of *koofuku-datta*.

Saying *Yoshida-san, koofuku-soo-desu-ne* sounds as if receiving that single ticket was enough to make Miss Yoshida's life happy forever; it can be used with a humorous effect, but otherwise it's not appropriate.

The English word "happy" does not have a Japanese equivalent in situational expressions like "I'm happy to meet you" or "I'm happy to be able to talk to you (said at the beginning of a speech)." Usually completely different expressions are used in such situations; it is not wise to simply replace "happy" with *ureshii or koofuku.*

A use of *kore-wa* (this is)

Yesterday afternoon Mr. Lerner saw an old gentleman trying to pick up his things in the hall of his apartment building. It seemed he had dropped his suitcase. Mr. Lerner ran up to help him. The old man thanked him saying

Kore-wa doomo arigatoo-gozaimasu.

Mr. Lerner understood that this was a polite expression of gratitude, but he wondered what *kore-wa* (*lit.* this is) stands for.

* * *

The old man could have just said *Doomo arigatoo-gozaimasu* too. The phrase *kore-wa* is sometimes used for emphasis; it usually expresses surprise. One often says

Kore-wa kore-wa.
これは　これは。
(Oh my! — *lit.* This is, this is.)

upon receiving an unexpected visitor or a gift. Or, when thanking someone for an unexpected kindness,

Kore-wa doomo sumimasen.
これは　どうも　すみません。

is used to mean "It's very kind of you. Thank you." In an apology too, one sometimes says

Kore-wa doomo shitsuree-shimashita.

to mean "I am terribly sorry."

42

Expressions of thanks or apology with *kore-wa* sound rather formal, and middle-aged or elderly men use them more often than young people. But young people also use this type of *kore-wa* to express surprise or strong emotion.

If it suddenly starts raining, one might say

Kore-wa komatta. Kasa-ga nai.
これは　こまった。かさが　ない。

(What a nuisance! I have no umbrella with me.)

Sometimes *kore-wa* is pronounced *korya*:

Korya ikenai. Moo konna jikan-da.
(Oh no! It's this late already.)

. . . *ni* . . . *ni* (A and B and C)

Mr. Lerner was driving in the city yesterday afternoon and was caught in a traffic jam. When he looked up at the overhead bridge above him, he saw a sign saying

Mamorimasu, sokudo-ni beruto-ni shakan-kyori.
守ります、速度に　ベルトに　車間距離。
(We will observe the speed limit, wear seat belts, and maintain a distance between cars.)

He understood what it meant and thought it was a clever phrase, but he wondered if . . . *ni* is the same as . . . *to.*

*   *   *

The particle *ni* is used to connect two or more nouns or pronouns as in

Iroirona mono-o kaimashita, hon-ni zasshi-ni jisho-ni . . .
(I bought various things — books, magazines, dictionaries, and so on.)

Other words used to connect two or more nouns or pronouns are *to, ya* and *toka.* The particle *to* is different from *ya* and *toka* in that it implies that everything has been named. In other words, saying

Tanaka-san-to Yamada-san-ga kimashita.
(Mr. Tanaka and Ms. Yamada came.)

means just the two people came. On the other hand saying

Tanaka-san-ya Yamada-san-ga kimashita.

44

means Tanaka-san, Yamada-san and some other people came: Tanaka-san and Yamada-san are given as examples. *Toka* is used in the same way, but it sounds more familiar than *ya*.

Unlike these three particles, *ni* can be used either when the speaker mentions everything or when he implies that there are some more not named. When it is used as in A-*ni* B-*ni* C, as in the safety slogan that Mr. Lerner saw, it implies that everything has been mentioned. When it is used as in A-*ni* B-*ni* C-*ni*. . ., the speaker implies that there are some more that have not been mentioned.

But the most important characteristic of *ni* is that it gives the impression that the speaker is naming things one after another in an impressive or dramatic way. Because of this, it is often used in set phrases or campaign slogans.

Expressions meaning 'but'

Mr. Lerner and Mr. Takada were explaining their project to Mr. Mori, the director of the company, and several other executives. Since Mr. Takada was speaking in formal language, Mr. Lerner also tried to sound formal. When modifying Mr. Takada's explanation, he said

> *Dakedo kore-wa kiwamete konnan-de-arimasu.*
> だけど
> (But this is extremely difficult.)

Everyone seemed to understand, but later Mr. Takada said that he should have used *shikashi* instead of *dakedo* to mean "but."

* * *

When speaking on formal occasions, one's wording must also be formal. Of the several expressions meaning "but," *shikashi* sounds formal and is often used in written language. Mr. Takada was right because the rest of Mr. Lerner's sentence — *kiwamete* (extremely), *konnan* (difficult) and . . . *de-arimasu* (is) — was quite formal in tone. Thus, he should have said

> *Shikashi kore-wa kiwamete konnan-de-arimasu.*
> しかし

When one does not have to be so formal, one can also use *desu-ga,* accompanied by slight changes in the rest of the sentence:

> *Desu-ga kore-wa hijoo-ni muzukashii koto-desu.*
> ですが

46

Desu-kedo can also be used in polite speech, although it sounds more conversational than *desu-ga*:

> *Desu-kedo, kore-wa taihen muzukashii-n-desu.*
> ですけど

In informal conversation, *demo* and *dakedo* can be used when one does not have to be polite:

> *Demo kore-wa totemo muzukashii-ne. . . .*
> でも

Shikashi, desu-ga, desu-kedo, demo and *dakedo* are all used to mean "but" with differences in the degree of formality, but one should be careful when using *datte. Datte* is often used in defending oneself:

> *Datte, kore-wa totemo muzukashii-n-desu-yo.*
> だって

can imply something like "You are telling me to do this, but it is so difficult that you shouldn't force me to." It can thus sound emotional and impolite.

Ohayoo-gozaimasu (Good morning)

Miss Winters, a friend of Mr. Lerner's, recently got a job at a broadcasting station. When she saw him last Saturday, she told him about an interesting experience she had there. She regularly works evenings, and when she first went to work, one of the Japanese there greeted her, saying

Ohayoo-gozaimasu.　お早うございます。

She said that it was already 4 o'clock, and wasn't it strange to say "Good morning?" The man immediately said she was right and said

Konnichiwa.　こんにちは。
(Good afternoon.)

She wondered why the man so readily corrected himself upon hearing criticism from a foreigner who does not speak Japanese well.

*   *   *

Ohayoo-gozaimasu literally means "It's early," and is usually used in the morning, but it is sometimes used regardless of the hour.

While *Ohayoo-gozaimasu* and *Oyasumi-nasai* (Good night) are used among family members as well as with those not related, *Konnichiwa* and *Konbanwa* (Good evening) are used only with non-family members.

At some work places, people regard other workers as similar to family members and consequently avoid using expressions that are used only with non-family members. Naturally, at such places *Konnichiwa* and *Konbanwa* are not used; *Ohayoo-gozaimasu* is used instead, at any hour of the day or night. In other places, people greet each other with *Konnichiwa* when meeting in the afternoon, since they regard other employees as individuals that are not at all like family members.

When Miss Winters said that *Ohayoo-gozaimasu* was strange, the man chose to change his expression rather than going to the trouble of explaining the reason why he had used *Ohayoo-gozaimasu*. To explain this sort of thing is troublesome for most Japanese; they usually choose what seems to be easier for foreigners to understand. Probably the man thought to himself, "Well, after all, she is a foreigner."

Uses of *toka* (and)

Miss Yoshida recently asked Mr. Kobayashi, the youngest person in the office, if he had a driver's license. He said that he had almost finished driving school, and added

Dakedo, mada shiken-toka ukenakucha.
(But I still have to take the tests.)

Mr. Lerner wondered why he had said *shiken-toka* instead of *shiken-o*. He thought *toka* meant ''or'' or ''and.''

*　　　*　　　*

The particle . . . *toka* (. . . and, such as . . .) is used in giving examples, as in

Biiru-toka hamu-toka iroiro katta.
ビールとか　ハムとか　いろいろ　買つた。
(I bought many things such as beer and ham.)
Suugaku-toka eego-toka, benkyoo-ga isogashii.
(I'm busy studying such things as math and English.)

In this usage, it is similar to *ya*; you can replace *toka* in the above with *ya*. Compared with *ya*, however, *toka* is more familiar.

Among young people today, *toka* seems to be used even when nothing else is implied. When Mr. Kobayashi said *shiken-toka ukenakucha*, he probably did not have anything in mind except the tests. Likewise, young people use *toka* as in

Ashita-no yuugata-toka-ni awanai?
(Why don't we meet tomorrow evening?)

Sono mae-ni denwa-toka kakete-ne.
その　前に　電話とか　かけてね。
(Call me before that, will you?)

Similar expressions like *demo* and *nado* are used to indicate the speaker's consideration toward the listener when asking a favor or issuing an invitation, as in

Ocha-demo nomimasen-ka.
(How about a cup of tea?)
Kore-nado ikaga-desu-ka.
(How would you like this?)

It is difficult to say for sure whether *toka* is used with the same implication or without such consideration, but we can say that young people seem to use *toka* in many cases because they prefer indirect expressions to precise statements.

O added to adjectives

Mr. Lerner went to visit Professor Takahashi the other day. When he was leaving after an hour's talk with the Takahashis, Mrs. Takahashi said

Mata o-chikai uchi-ni doozo.
また　お近い　うちに　どうぞ。

Mr. Lerner understood that this meant "Please come again soon." He knew the expression *chikai uchi* (before long, *lit.* within a near time), but he hadn't realized that *chikai* can be made polite with the prefix *o*, and wondered if many other adjectives are used this way.

*   *   *

The polite prefix *o* is usually added to nouns, as in *o-taku* (your house) and *o-shigoto* (your work). It is also added to adjectives that refer to someone's condition, as in

wakai: Ano sensee-wa o-wakai-desu-ne.
　　　　　　　　　　　お若い
　　　　(That instructor is young.)
hayai: Kyoo-wa o-hayai-desu-ne.
　　　　　　　　お早い
　　　　(You're early today.)
isogashii: Itsumo o-isogashisoo-desu-ne.
　　　　(You always seem to be busy.)

In very polite speech, *o* is added to set phrases like *chikai uchi-ni* (before long) as in Mrs. Takahashi's sentence above. *O* is also used in referring to the weather or general social conditions as in

O-atsuku narimashita-ne.

お暑く　なりましたね。
(It has become hot, hasn't it?)
Nandemo o-takaku narimashita.
(Everything has become expensive.)

In these examples, *o* does not directly refer to someone's condition, but it still concerns the listener or human beings in general. When an adjective has no relation to human life, *o* is not added. It would be strange to say something like

Fujisan-wa hontoo-ni o-takai-desu-ne.
(Mount Fuji is really high.)

Chuu (while) and *juu* (all through)

When Mr. Lerner called Mr. Okada at his office yesterday morning, his secretary answered

> *Ima kaigi-chuu-desu.*
> いま　会議中です。
> (He is in conference now.)

and added

> *Gozen-chuu-niwa owarimasu-ga.*
> 午前中には　おわりますが。
> (It will be over before noon.)

Mr. Lerner was interested in the use of . . .*chuu*, which seemed to be used for both action and time; he also wondered if . . .*juu* is used in the same way.

*　　*　　*　　*

The suffix *chuu* is added to nouns indicating actions, as in *shigoto-chuu* (while at work) and *unten-chuu* (while driving).

> *Shigoto-chuu-wa tabako-wa suimasen.*
> (I don't smoke while at work.)
> *Unten-chuu-ni hoka-no koto-wa kangaenai hoo-ga ii.*
> (We had better not think about other things while driving.)

To give a few of the most common expressions with *chuu*, *kaigi-chuu* (in conference), *choosa-chuu* (under investigation) and *ohanashi-chuu* (the line is busy — *lit.* someone is talking) are often used.

Chuu is sometimes used with a period of time

54

as in *gozen-chuu* (during the morning) and *konshuu-chuu* (this week).

> *Raishuu-chuu-ni ojama-shimasu.*
> (I will come to see you some time next week.)

On the other hand, . . .*juu* is mainly added to nouns indicating a certain place or space and gives the meaning of "all over":

> *Uwasa-ga machi-juu-ni hirogatta.*
> うわさが　町じゅうに　ひろがった。
> (The rumor spread all over town.)
> *Karada-juu-ga itai.*
> (I feel pain all over my body.)

In some set expressions . . .*juu* is added to nouns referring to time and gives the meaning of "all through":

> *Kinoo-wa ichinichi-juu ame-ga futta.*
> 一日じゅう
> (It rained all day yesterday.)
> *Ichinen-juu hana-ga saite-iru.*
> 一年じゅう
> (Flowers bloom all through the year.)

Ookii and *ookina* (big)

Mr. Lerner attended a meeting at which several new projects were discussed by senior members of the company.

When Mr. Lerner asked Mr. Mori about a possible improvement in management, Mr. Mori answered that he needed some time to think about it, and added

>   *Nanishiro ookii mondai-da-kara.*
>   (Since it is a big problem.)

Mr. Lerner understood, but he wondered whether *ookina* could also be used instead of *ookii*. When he came to think about it, these two words seemed very confusing to him.

*   *   *

Ookina (big) and *chiisana* (small) are used only before nouns whereas *ookii* (big) and *chiisai* (small) can be used either before nouns or at the end of a sentence.

(1)   *Kono mondai-wa ookii.*
      この　問題は　大きい。
      (This problem is big.)
(2)   *Kore-wa ookii mondai-desu.*
      (This is a big problem.)
(3)   *Kore-wa ookina mondai-desu.*
      (This is a big problem.)

Sentences (2) and (3) are both used, but many people seem to prefer (3). The small difference in meaning between *ookina* and *ookii* is that *ookina* is often preferred to *ookii* with abstract words. In the

case of *mondai* both can be used, but in the following examples *ookina* is used:

> *Kaisha-no tame-ni ookina kooseki-o ageta.*
> 　　　　　　　　大きな　功績
> (He made a great achievement for his compa-
ny.)
> *Kagaku-gijutsu-wa saikin ookina shinpo-o togeta.*
> 　　　　　　　　　　大きな　進歩
> (Scientific technology has recently made great
progress.)

In the above cases *ookii* is not usually used.

The same difference is seen with *chiisana* and
chiisai:

> *Chiisana machigai-wa ki-ni shinai koto-da.*
> (You shouldn't worry about small mistakes.)
> *Chiisai toki-wa otonashii kodomo-deshita.*
> (He was a quiet child when he was small.)

Okusan and *Yoshiko-san*

Mr. Lerner had not visited the Takadas for a few weeks, and so he asked Mr. Takada about his wife yesterday, saying

Yoshiko-san, genki-desu-ka. (How is Yoshiko?)

Mr. Takada looked unpleasantly surprised, and then said

Ee, genki-desu-yo. (She's fine.)

Mr. Lerner had known Mrs. Takada for so long that he thought he should refer to her by her first name rather than by *okusan* (your wife), but Mr. Takada did not seem to like it.

* * *

Using someone's first name when referring to or addressing him/her is much more limited in Japanese than in English. It is common for a Japanese to say to his/her colleagues things like

Okusan, genki?
おくさん、元気？
(Is your wife fine?)
Musuko-san, gookaku omedetoo.
むすこさん、合格　おめでとう。

(Congratulations on your son's success on his test.)

First names are used between people who used them when they first met. Kindergarten children usually use first names among themselves, and when they grow up, they often retain the habit. First names are often used between childhood

58

friends, even when they are in middle or old age, except on formal occasions.

In English, when two people have become good friends, they use first names to address each other, but in Japanese, the initial pattern usually continues without change. If an English-speaking person starts using first names to address or refer to Japanese acquaintances without being asked to do so, many will be surprised unless they are familiar with the English custom in this respect. Sometimes a Japanese may even feel offended at being addressed by his or her first name. Mr. Takada probably felt that Mr. Lerner was being too personal when he said *Yoshiko-san* instead of *okusan*.

Chuushi-suru (call off) and *chuushi-ni naru* (be called off)

When Mr. Lerner and his colleagues were having coffee yesterday afternoon, Miss Yoshida said that she was going to buy a ticket for a concert by a singer she liked very much. Then Mr. Takada said

> *Aa, are chuushi-ni natta-soo-dayo.*
> 中止に なったそうだよ
> (I heard that it has been called off.)

She looked shocked and said

> *Chuushi-suru-nante hidoi.*
> 中止するなんて ひどい。
> (What a thing to do, to call it off.)

Mr. Lerner wondered why neither of the two used *chuushi-sareru* to mean "be called off.

*　　　*　　　*

Verbs consisting of kanji compounds and *suru* are often used in "kanji compound plus *ni naru*" form as in

> *chuushi-ni naru* (to be called off, suspended)
> *enki-ni naru* (to be postponed)
> *haishi-ni naru* (to be abolished)
> *kaisee-ni naru* (to be revised)

This form sounds neutral and is preferred in formal speech or written language; TV news announcers usually use this form.

On the other hand, . . .*suru* is more conversational and is used in daily speech. *Suru* is especially used when one wants to emphasize that someone is responsible for an action. Miss Yoshida used *chuu-*

shi-suru because she was critical of those who had decided to call off the concert.

The form . . .*sareru* is not commonly used in speech; it is usually used in written language. When it is used in daily conversation, it often implies that the speaker is affected by the action, as in

Kyuu-ni chuushi-sareru-nante meewaku-da.

(Calling it off so suddenly means big trouble for me.)

Gachi (be apt to, tend to)

During lunch hour yesterday Miss Yoshida looked at the newspaper and said

Toobun kumori-gachi-desu-tte.
くもりがち
(It says it will tend to be cloudy for some days to come.)

as if disappointed. Mr. Lerner remembered that she had wanted to go hiking over the weekend, so he said

Shuumatsu-niwa hare-gachi-ni narimasu-yo.
(We should have fine weather during the weekend.)

Miss Yoshida thanked him for his encouraging remark, but said that *hare-gachi* sounded strange.

*　　　*　　　*

Gachi, which means "be apt to" or "tend to," is added to nouns or the stem of verbs (the form used before *-masu*) as in

Kono basu-wa itsumo okure-gachi-desu-ne.
おくれがち
(The bus on this route often comes late.)
Yuugata ame-ga yamu-to kasa-o wasure-gachi-da.
忘れがち
(When it clears up in the evening, people tend to forget their umbrellas.)

This suffix is usually added to words with a negative implication; you can say *kumori-gachi* (tend to be cloudy) and *wasure-gachi* (tend to forget), but you cannot say such things as *hare-gachi* (tend to be fine) or *oboe-gachi* (tend to remember). *Gachi* is most commonly added to the stem of verbs that imply failure to reach a desired goal, as in *okure-gachi* (tend to be behind).

Following is a list of some other common uses of *gachi*:

ayamatta handan-ni ochiiri-gachi
(*lit.* tend to fall into the wrong judgment)
henken-ni toraware-gachi
(*lit.* tend to be prejudiced)
hito-ni tayori-gachi
(*lit.* tend to depend on others)

. . . *ni totte* (for . . .)

Mr. Okada came to have a business discussion with Mr. Lerner yesterday afternoon. After he left, Mr. Lerner noticed that he had forgotten some of his papers. Miss Yoshida said she would call Mr. Okada's secretary and tell her about it. Mr. Lerner thanked her and commented

Okada-san-ni taishite taisetsuna mono-deshoo-kara.

(Since it must be very valuable to Mr. Okada.)

She agreed, but later told him that he should have used *ni totte* instead of *ni taishite*.

*　　*　　*

ni totte is used to indicate that something is of value, interest or advantage to a person.

Kono tokee-wa watashi-ni totte taisetsuna mono-
　　　　　　わたしに　とって　大切な　もの
desu.

(This watch is very valuable to me — a keepsake, etc.)

Kono hon-wa kodomo-ni totte-wa omoshiroku nai-daroo.

(This book may not be interesting to young people.)

Watashi-ni totte-wa hajimete-no keeken-desu.
わたしに　とっては　はじめての　経験

(It is my first experience with it.)

It is used in such expressions as

. . . ni totte yasashii/muzukashii
(easy/difficult for . . .)

> . . . *ni totte tsugoo-ga ii/warui*
> (convenient/inconvenient for . . .)
> . . . *ni totte arigatai/meewaku-da*
> (profitable, welcome/unwelcome for . . .)

Foreigners tend to use *ni taishite* when *ni totte* should be used. *Ni taishite* is used as in:

> *Ano-hito-ni taishite sonna shitsureena koto-o itte-wa ikenai.*
> (You shouldn't say such an impolite thing to him.)
> *Shain-wa shachoo-no yarikata-ni taishite fuman-o kanjite-iru.*
> (The employees feel dissatisfied with the president's way of doing things.)

Namely *ni taishite* is used, to refer to the object of an action or relation. It is wrong to say things like *kore-wa watashi-ni taishite muzukashii* or *kodomo-ni taishite omoshiroku nai.*

Hazukashigariya (a shy person)

Yesterday at noon, Miss Yoshida hurried out of the office before anyone could ask her to go out for lunch. That afternoon she said that her brother had come by and wanted to have lunch with her. Her colleagues said she should have brought him to the office so that they could meet him, but she said she could not have, and added

Totemo hazukashigariya-desu-kara.

Mr. Lerner understood that her brother did not want to meet people at the office, but he could not catch the long word she had used to describe him.

* * *

Expressions referring to feelings like *ureshii*, *kanashii* and *hazukashii* are usually used in reference to the speaker, and when referring to someone else's feelings several other expressions are used. One is to add . . . *to itte-imasu* as in

Otooto-wa ureshii-to itte-imasu.
(My brother said he's very happy about it.)

Another is to replace the last "*i*" sound with *soo*:

Takada-san-wa ureshisoo-desu.
(Mr. Takada looks happy.)

A third way is to replace the last "*i*" with *garu*:

Imooto wa kanashi-gatte-imasu.
(My sister is sad.)
Otooto-wa shiranai hito-ni au-no-o hazukashi-garu.

(My brother feels shy when meeting someone for the first time.)

Words with *garu* like *hazukashi-garu* are sometimes changed into nouns which mean "a person who feels . . ." by replacing the last "*ru*" with "*ri-ya*."

sabishii (lonely) — *sabishi-garu* (feel lonely) — *sabishigari-ya* さびしがりや (a person who often feels very lonely)
hazukashii (shy, embarrassed) — *hazukashi-garu* (be shy) — *hazukashigari-ya* はずかしがりや (a person who is very shy)

This pattern is limited in use; one cannot use it freely with just any adjective.

There are several other words ending in *gari-ya*, although they do not exactly refer to a person's feelings:

atarashigari-ya
(a person who is very fond of new styles)
mendookusagari-ya
(a person who dislikes bothering with details)

All these words have a slightly teasing implication, although not malicious, and should not be used when referring to someone politely.

Gomen (Pardon)

Mr. Lerner and Mr. Takada went out for lunch together yesterday, but the restaurant they went to was unusually full then. The waiter said they would have to wait about 30 minutes. Mr. Takada immediately said

Sonna-ni matasareru-nowa gomen-dana.

and proposed to Mr. Lerner that they go to another restaurant. Mr. Lerner understood that he did not want to wait, but he could not exactly understand the meaning of the word *gomen*.

*　　　*　　　*

The word *gomen* literally means "your pardon." When it is used before *da* or *desu*, it means "I would like to have your pardon to be spared of it." By *Sonna-ni matasareru-nowa gomen-dana*, Mr. Takada meant "I would like to be excused from being kept waiting so long." In the same way one often says things like

Kono toshi-de shiken-o ukeru-nowa gomen-desu-yo.
この　年で　試験を　うけるのは　ごめんですよ。
(Someone as old as me shouldn't be taking exams.)
Ano mise-wa gomen-da. Kanji-ga warui-kara.
(I don't want to go to that shop. It's very unpleasant there.)

Probably the most common usage of *gomen* is in the expression *Gomen-nasai*. This means "Excuse me" or "Sorry," and is used in rather familiar speech. Sometimes *gomen* is used alone, mostly by men, in familiar conversation:

> *Osoku natte, gomen.*　おそくなって、ごめん。
> (Sorry I'm late.)

A similar expression, *Gomen-kudasai*, is also used to express apology, but this sounds polite, and is used mainly in such cases as calling for attention at someone's door or when parting from someone.

> *Gomen-kudasai. Yoshida-san-no otaku-wa kochira-deshoo-ka.*
> (Excuse me. Is this where Miss Yoshida lives?)
> *Dewa kore-de shitsuree-shimasu. Gomen-kudasai.*
> (I'll take my leave now. Goodbye.)

Unlike *Gomen-nasai*, this is not used for asking to be pardoned for having done something rude. When one has accidentally stepped on someone's foot, for instance, one should say *Sumimasen* (Excuse me), *Gomen-nasai* or *Shitsuree-shimashita* (I'm very sorry). It would be strange to say *Gomen-kudasai* in this case.

Darake (filled with)

Yesterday afternoon Miss Yoshida started taking some files down from the top shelf of the bookcase in the office. Mr. Lerner offered to help, but she said she could do it herself, adding

Hokori-darake-desu-kara.
ほこりだらけ
(Since they are covered with dust.)

He understood that when he saw that she was wearing an apron to protect her dress, but the expression . . . *darake* was new to him. He wondered if he could say something like

Toori-wa hito-darake-desu.
(The streets are full of people.)

*　　　*　　　*

The suffix *darake* is added to nouns to mean "filled with," but you cannot say *Toori-wa hito-darake-desu* because *darake* implies that something or someone is covered with undesirable matter or is damaged by something. Thus it is most common to use it in the following way:

Heya-juu hokori-darake-da.
(The whole room is covered with dust.)
Kuruma-ga doro-darake-ni natta.
どろだらけ
(The car is covered with mud.)
Watashi-no eego-wa machigai-darake-desu.
間違いだらけ
(I always make mistakes when I use English
— *lit.* My English is full of mistakes.)

Kega-o shite chi-darake-ni natta hito-ga mieta.

(I could see someone injured and bleeding a lot.)

To say that something is filled with something neutral, not unpleasant, you can say . . . *de ippai* as in

Omatsuri-de machi-wa hito-de ippai-ni natta.
人で いっぱい

(There was a festival and the town was full of people.)

Me-ga namida-de ippai-ni natta.
(My eyes were filled with tears.)

Darake is familiar and not used in formal speech or writing; . . . *de ippai* can be used in both familiar and polite conversation. There are several other expressions for use in writing which mean "be filled with":

yorokobi/kanashimi-ni michita kao
(a face filled with joy/sorrow)
Kangee-no hitobito-ga endoo-o umetsukushita.
(Welcoming people filled the street where he went.)

71

Kagi-ga kakatte-imasu
(It's locked)

Mr. Lerner went early to the office on Monday morning because he had left something unfinished over the weekend. But when he arrived, the door was locked. While he was looking for the key in his pocket, Miss Yoshida came and said

A, kagi-ga kakatte-imasu-ne. (Oh, it's locked.)

He said yes and unlocked the door, but while opening the door for her, he wondered if one can also say

Kagi-ga kakerarete-imasu-ne.

* * *

To mean "to lock the door," one says *kagi-o kakeru* as in

Heya-o deru toki-wa kanarazu kagi-o kakete-kudasai.

(Please be sure to lock the door when you leave the room.)

Kesa kagi-o kakeru-no-o wasureta yoona ki-ga suru.

(I feel that I might have forgotten to lock the door when I left this morning.)

But when describing a door that is locked, it is common to say *kagi-ga kakatte-iru.*

In daily conversation passive expressions such as *kagi-ga kakerareru*, and *dentoo-ga kesareru* (the light is turned off) are not commonly used. Instead, intransitive verbs like *kakaru* and *kieru* (to go out, be turned off) are usually used. It is wise to learn the most common expressions of this type to avoid sounding stiff.

> *terebi-ga tsuite-iru* (the TV is on)
> テレビが　ついている
> *to-ga shimatte-iru* (the door is closed)
> *mado-ga aite-iru* (the window is open)
> まどが　あいている
> *heya-ga katazuite-iru* (the room is tidied up)
> へやが　かたづいている

You can use . . . *te-aru* with transitive verbs as in

> *terebi-ga tsukete-aru* (the TV is on)
> テレビが　つけてある
> *to-ga shimete-aru* (the door is closed)
> *mado-ga akete-aru* (the window is open)
> *heya-ga katazukete-aru* (the room is tidied up)

These expressions are also common in daily conversation. The difference is that they imply that you are interested in some way in who took the action. The interest may come from gratitude, but it may be taken as dissatisfaction or a reprimand.

. . .*mono* used to make expressions indirect

Yesterday afternoon Mr. Okada came to have a business discussion with Mr. Lerner and Mr. Takada. During the discussions Mr. Okada presented a proposal to change their original plan and asked for their opinions, saying

Donna mon-deshoo-ka.
どんな　もんでしょうか。
(I wonder what you think of it.)

Mr. Lerner understood this sentence, but wondered what the word *mono* means, and if *Doo-deshoo-ka* can also be used.

*　　　*　　　*

The word *mono* (*lit*. thing) and its shortened form *mon*, have several usages, and one is to make expressions indirect. Mr. Okada could have simply said

Doo-desu-ka.
(What do you think? — *lit*. How is it?)

or

Doo-deshoo-ka.
(What would you think? — more reserved than *Doo-desu-ka*.)

Adding *mon* to sentences does not change their meaning, but makes them sound more indirect and often more reserved or refined. When *mon*, a noun, is used after *doo*, *doo* changes into *donna*. *Mono* or *mon* are used in such expressions as

Ikagana mono-deshoo-ka.
いかがな　ものでしょうか。

74

(What would you think about it? — very polite)

Moo sukoshi yasuku naranai mon-deshoo-ka.

(Would it be possible to reduce the price a little?)

Konna shigoto, yametai mono-desu.

(I would like to quit this kind of job, if possible.)

Soo negaitai mono-desu.

そう　願いたい　ものです。

(I wish they would do that.)

When asking someone's advice with *mon(o)*, verbs are often used in the past tense:

Doo shita mon-deshoo-ka.

(What would you suggest I do?)

Dare-ni tanonda mono-deshoo-ne.

(Whom would you suggest I ask to do it?)

Ikura-gurai haratta mon-deshoo-ka.

(How much would you suggest I pay?)

Amari . . . nai (not . . . much) (1)

While having coffee during their break yesterday afternoon, people started talking about how they had spent their childhood. Mr. Takada asked Mr. Lerner if he had studied hard. He answered

Yoku benkyoo-shimasen-deshita.

to mean "I didn't study much." Everybody understood, but Miss Yoshida said he should have used *amari* instead of *yoku* with the negative ending. He thanked her for her correction, but later wondered why people often say *Yoku wakarimasen* (I don't understand well).

*　　　*　　　*

The word *yoku* has two usages; one means "well" or "skillfully" as in

Tenisu-ga yoku dekimasu.
(He plays tennis well.)
Chuugokugo-ga yoku hanasemasu.
(He speaks Chinese well.)

Another usage means "much of," "frequently" as in

Kinoo-wa yoku furimashita-ne.
(It rained a lot yesterday, didn't it?)
Kare, yoku taberu-nee.
(He eats a lot!)
Ano mise-wa yoku ikimasu.
(I often go to that store.)

In the first usage, *yoku* can be used with negative verbs, as in

76

Tenisu-wa yoku dekimasen.
テニスは　よく　できません。
(I cannot play tennis well.)
Chuugokugo-wa yoku hanasemasen.
(I cannot speak Chinese well.)

With the second usage, however, *amari* is used with negation:

Kono-goro-wa amari furimasen-ne.
このごろは　あまり　降りませんね。
(We don't have much rain these days.)
Ano mise-wa amari ikimasen, tooi-node.
(I don't go to that store very often: it's rather far.)

To mean "I didn't study much," Mr. Lerner should have said *Amari benkyoo-shimasen-deshita.* Saying *Yoku benkyoo-shimasen-deshita* can be understood but sounds foreign. When a Japanese has heard

Yoku benkyoo . . .

he expects the sentence to end in the affirmative. If the speaker then says *shimasen-deshita,* the listener will feel it somehow awkward.

Eki-made aruku
(walk as far as the station)

Yesterday afternoon Mr. Lerner's colleagues talked during their coffee break about ~~how much time they spend commuting~~. Miss Yoshida said she has to take a bus to the nearest railway station. Mr. Lerner said

Watashi-wa eki-e arukimasu.

to mean "I walk to the station." Then Mr. Takada said

Boku-mo eki-made aruku-yo.
(I walk to the station, too.)

Mr. Lerner wondered if saying *eki-e aruku* was wrong.

*   *   *

The verb *aruku* refers to the action of walking a certain distance, but it does not include reaching a certain place. Thus, it is common to say

Mainichi go-kiro-gurai arukimasu.
(I walk about 5 km every day.)
Uchi-kara eki-made arukimasu.
(I walk from my house to the station.)

but it sounds strange to say *eki-e aruku* or *uchi-e aruku*. Where you would say in English "I walk to the station," one says in Japanese

Eki-made arukimasu.　駅まで　歩きます。

Several other verbs are also used in a similar way:

Osoku natta-node eki-made hashitta.
(I ran to the station since I was late.)
Mukoo-gishi-made oyogimasu.
(I will swim to the other side of the river.)

In the above cases, one does not usually say *eki-e hashitta* or *mukoo-gishi-e oyogimasu* because *hashiru* and *oyogu* do not refer to moving toward a destination.

The verbs mentioned above can be used with . . .*te iku/kaeru* to mean "reach a destination by . . .ing."

Eki-ewa chikai-kara aruite ikimasu.
　　　　　　歩いて　行きます
(Since the station is fairly close, I walk there.)
Ureshikatta-node hashitte uchi-e kaetta.
　　　　　　走って　うちへ　帰った
(I was so happy that I ran home.)

Expressions meaning 'should have'

Miss Yoshida brought a homemade cake to the office the other day. During the afternoon break she cut it and everyone had started eating when Mr. Okada came in. She said it was too bad that there was none left for him, and Mr. Lerner added

Gofun hayaku kuru-beki-deshita.

to mean "You should have come five minutes earlier." Everybody agreed, but she said *kureba yokatta-noni* would have sounded better.

* * *

Beki is a rather literary expression used to refer to moral obligations as in

Wareware-wa heewa-o mamoru tame-ni doryoku-suru-beki-da.
(We should make efforts to maintain peace.)

Beki is not appropriate in the case above, as Miss Yoshida said. When someone has missed something good by coming too late, one usually says

Motto hayaku kureba yokatta-noni.
もっと 早く 来れば よかったのに。
(You should have come earlier, or, If only you had come earlier.)

Eba literally means "if one does/did" and *yokatta* means "was good" or "would have been good"; *noni* means "although." Thus the whole thing literally means "Although you should have come earlier, you didn't."

This *eba yokatta* form is used when referring to other actions and other people, as in

   Kasa-o motte-kureba yokatta.
   かさを　持ってくれば　よかった。
   (I should have brought my umbrella with me, or, I wish I had brought an umbrella with me.)
   Hayaku yamereba yokatta(-noni).
   (He should have stopped doing it earlier.)

With the negative, *nakereba* is used:

   Konna kaisha-ni hairanakereba yokatta.
   (I shouldn't have entered such a company as this.)

Noni is added at the end when the speaker wants to emphasize regret or criticism. Miss Yoshida probably thought of using . . . *eba yokatta-noni* because she regretted that Mr. Okada had missed this chance for a treat. It can sound accusatory depending on the situation; to a person who has dropped an expensive vase on the floor, the owner may say angrily

   Ki-o tsukete hakobeba yokatta-noni.
   (You should have been more careful carrying it.)

. . .*no koto* meaning 'about . . .'

During his coffee break yesterday, Mr. Lerner was thinking about his sister Margaret, who had not written him recently. Miss Yoshida noticed this and asked what he was thinking so hard about. He answered

Imooto-ni tsuite kangaete-imasu.

meaning "I'm thinking about my sister." She said

Imooto-san-no koto? Nanika atta-n-desu-ka?
(About your sister? Has something happened to her?)

Later he wondered if . . . *ni tsuite kangaeru* sounded strange.

*   *   *

To mean "to think about someone," one usually says . . . *no koto-o kangaeru/omou* ······の こと を 考える／思う . The expression *ni tsuite* is not commonly used with daily matters, especially concerning a person. A lecturer might say something like

Kyoo-wa booeki-mondai-ni tsuite ohanashi-shimasu.
(Today I'm going to discuss trade problems.)

But in daily conversation *no koto* is commonly used, as in

Arubaito-no koto, umaku itta-yo.
(The problems with my part-time job have been taken care of.)
Shiken-no koto-ga shinpai-de yoku nemuremasen.

試験の　ことが　心配で……

(I'm so worried about the exam that I can't sleep well.)

In the examples above, . . . *ni tsuite* would sound strange.

Especially when expressing an attitude toward someone, *no koto* is mainly used as in

Ano-hito-no koto-wa doomo suki-ni narenai.
あの人の　ことは　どうも　好きに　なれない。
(Somehow I don't like him at all.)
Kare, okusan-no koto(-o) totemo daiji-ni shite-imasu.
(He loves his wife very much — *lit*. He thinks much of his wife.)

Dattara meaning 'if that is the case'

Miss Yoshida looked tired yesterday afternoon. Mr. Takada noticed and asked her if she was all right. She answered that she had caught a cold. Mr. Takada said

Dattara moo kaettara?
だったら　もう　帰ったら？
(Then why don't you go home now?)

She thanked him and left work early. Mr. Lerner wondered what *dattara* by itself means.

* * *

Dattara literally means "if it is so." The ending . . . *tara* is used to indicate a condition, as in *ittara* (if you go, if you say) and *samukattara* (if it's cold). In the same way, *dattara* means "if that is the case"; you can also say *soo-dattara* to mean "if that is so," but very often *soo* is left out.

Dattara is used before stating an opinion or making a proposal, after receiving some information, as in

I. A: *Jitsu-wa ano-hito-ni susumerarete yatta-n-desu.*
    (To tell the truth, he recommended that I do it.)
   B: *Dattara kare-nimo sekinin-ga arimasu-yo.*
    (In that case he should take responsibility, too.)
II. A: *Ashita-wa tsugoo-ga warui-n-da-kedo.*
    (Tomorrow is not convenient for me.)
   B: *Dattara asatte-ni shiyoo-ka.*
    (Then shall we make it the day after tomorrow?)

Dattara sounds familiar and cannot be used with superiors. In polite speech one should use *de-shitara* instead. If Mr. Takada had been talking to Mr. Mori, the director of the company, for instance, instead of Miss Yoshida, he would have said something like

Deshitara moo okaeri-ni nattara ikaga-deshoo-ka.

でしたら もう お帰りに なったら いかがでしょうか。

(Then it might be better if you went home now.)

Ja (then) can be used in place of *dattara* in the earlier examples above, but *dattara* emphasizes the stating of one's opinion based on information one has received. You can say *Ja, sayoonara* じゃ、さようなら (Well, goodbye now), but you cannot say

Dattara sayoonara.

Hotondo meaning 'almost all'

The other day Mr. Lerner saw a tie which he liked very much at a department store and decided to buy it even though it was rather expensive. When he wore it to the office the next day, Miss Yoshida admired it lavishly. Mr. Takada also liked it and commented that it must have been very expensive, so he answered

Hotondo ichiman-en-deshita.

to mean "It was almost ¥10,000." Miss Yoshida said *hotondo* sounded strange in this case.

* * *

To mean that something cost almost ¥10,000, one usually says *Ichiman-en-chikaku shimashita. Hotondo* is not used to mean "almost" when preceding a word indicating price or number. It sounds strange to say things like

hotondo sanjissai (almost 30 years old)
hotondo goji (almost 5 o'clock)

However, when the number indicates an amount or span of time, *hotondo* can be used as in

Hotondo ichinichi-juu nete-ita.
(I was in bed almost all day long.)
Hotondo hitohako tabete-shimatta.
ほとんど　ひと箱　食べてしまった。
(I ate up almost one whole package of them.)

When *hotondo* is used before a verb, it actually means "almost all" rather than "almost" as in

86

Gakusee-wa hotondo inaku natta.

学生は ほとんど いなく なった。

(Almost all the students have left.)

Shigoto-wa hotondo owarimashita.

(I have finished up almost all of the work.)

Hotondo is used very often with the negative form of a verb; in this case *hotondo . . . nai* corresponds to the English "hardly/scarcely."

Kare-no hanashi-wa hotondo wakaranakatta.

彼の 話は ほとんど わからなかった。

(I could hardly understand a thing he said.)

Hotondo is not used before a verb, however, to mean "almost did . . ." as in "I almost stumbled." If you said

Hotondo korobimashita.

it would not mean "I almost stumbled"; instead it would mean "Almost all of them stumbled." To mean "I almost stumbled," one would say

Moo sukoshi-de korobu tokoro-deshita.

Kiita ato-de and *kiite-kara*
(after asking him)

Mr. Mori, the director of the company, came over to where Mr. Lerner and Miss Yoshida were talking and asked them the name of the restaurant where several colleagues had dined a few weeks before. They had spoken very highly of the restaurant and Mr. Mori wanted to know its name. But neither Mr. Lerner nor Miss Yoshida could remember it, so Mr. Lerner said

Takada-san-ni kiita ato-de oshirase-shimasu.
(I'll tell you after I ask Mr. Takada about it.)

After Mr. Mori left, Miss Yoshida said *kiite-kara* should have been used instead of *kiita ato-de*.

*   *   *

The two expressions *kiita ato-de* and *kiite-kara* are similar, but not quite the same. . . . *ta ato-de* is used to indicate that one action is taken after another, as in

Ginkoo-ni yotta ato-de yuubinkyoku-e itta.
銀行に　寄った　あとで　郵便局へ　行った。
(I went to the bank and then to the post office.)
Satoo-o ireta ato-de shooyu-o iremasu.
(Soy sauce is added after the sugar.)

Here, the speaker's concern is with the order of the two actions.

On the other hand, . . .*te-kara* usually implies that the second action is taken on the basis of the result of the first action; very often the first action is indispensable for the second. Saying

Takada-san-ni kiite-kara oshirase-shimasu.

88

高田さんに　きいてから　お知らせします。

implies that the speaker cannot provide information unless he asks Mr. Takada. Saying

> *Takada-san-ni kiita ato-de oshirase-shimasu.*

simply means that the speaker will ask Mr. Takada and later provide the information. In the same
way

> *Ano-hito-ga kite-kara kimemashoo.*
> (Let's decide after she comes.)

implies "we should not decide without asking her."
    Generally speaking, . . .*ta ato-de* tends to be
used in giving factual information whereas . . .*te-
kara* is used in expressing an idea or opinion.

Zeekin-o torareru
(to have to pay taxes)

Mr. Takada and several colleagues came back after lunch yesterday afternoon, and said that they had eaten at a sushi restaurant which had just opened a few days before, but were surprised at the high prices there. Mr. Takada said

Sanzen-en torareta.

which literally means "I was robbed of ¥3,000." Mr. Lerner was interested in this sentence, and remembered that people often use *torareru* with taxes.

*   *   *

Torareru is the passive form of *toru* (take, rob, steal). It is used to report an actual robbery as in

Doroboo-ni okane-o toraremashita.
(A thief took my money — *lit.* I had my money stolen by a thief.)

But *torareru* is also used when one dislikes having to pay a certain amount. Mr. Takada did not think the sushi he ate was worth ¥3,000, so he used this expression. One uses it when having to pay a surprisingly high price, as in

Sore, ikura torareta?
(How much did you have to pay for that?)
Kore, zuibun torareta-yo.
これ、ずいぶん　とられたよ。
(I had to pay quite a lot for this.)

With taxes, one often uses *harau* (pay) in conversation. The official term for paying taxes is *osameru*,

90

which means "to put something in where it should be," but this expression seems to be dying out in daily conversation, probably because people do not feel that taxes are going where they should. When one feels taxes are unduly high or it is unpleasant to pay them, *torareru* is used as in

> *Shoohi-zee-o torareru-nowa iya-desu-ne.*
> 消費税を　とられるのは　いやですね。
> (It's unpleasant to have to pay the consumption tax.)

Torareru is used for payments other than taxes, especially when the exact amount was not known beforehand:

> *Chuusha-ihan-de bakkin-o toraremashita.*
> 罰金を　とられました
> (I had to pay a fine for a parking violation.)
> *Saabisu-ryoo-o torareta-node takaku natta.*
> (I had to pay a lot because a service charge was added.)

Ya, a familiar sentence particle

Mr. Takada, who was reading a magazine at lunchtime yesterday, suddenly started laughing. He said

Kore-wa okashii-ya. (This is really funny.)

and handed the magazine to Mr. Lerner while pointing to a satirical cartoon. Mr. Lerner also found it funny, and said *Honto-desu-ne* (It really is), but he wondered what *ya* at the end of the sentence meant.

* * *

Several particles are added to the end of a sentence, as in *Ii otenki-desu-ne* (It's a fine day, isn't it?). *Ne* and *yo* are used in both polite and familiar conversation, but some are used only in familiar conversation, and *ya* is one of them. *Ya* is similar to *na* in function, but it is more familiar than *na* and women seldom use it.

One usage of *ya* is to emphasize one's feelings; Mr. Takada used it in this way in the case above. It is added to a monologuelike sentence as in

Kono koohii nurui-ya. Attamete-koyoo.
(This coffee is cold. I'll go and warm it.)
Baka-ni nemui-ya. Doo shita-n-daroo.
ばかに　ねむいや。どう　したんだろう。
(I'm awfully sleepy. What's the matter with me?)

In this usage, *ya* is added to expressions of emotions and states of things, not to actions. Namely, it is used after adjectives ending in "*i*" as in

Samui-ya. (I'm cold.)
Muzukashii-ya. (It's difficult.)

It can be added to the negative form of verbs because it describes conditions, not actions:

Yoku wakaranai-ya.
よく　わからないや。
(I don't understand it well.)
Moo ma-ni awanai-ya.
(I won't be in time.)

But it cannot follow verbs describing actions. It is not added to *na* adjectives either; one does not say *Taikutsu-ya* to mean "It's boring" in standard Japanese.

Another usage of *ya* is to emphasize suggestion of an action:

Moo yameyoo-ya. (Let's stop now.)
もう　やめようや。
Ashita-ni shiyoo-ya. (Let's do it tomorrow.)

This is also mainly used in men's familiar conversation.

Expressions used for praise

One of the employees at the company left last month after working there for 20 years. The director praised him in the presence of all the employees on the day when he bade him farewell, saying that he had never been absent or late during the long period of his employment. Later Miss Yoshida said

Honto-ni erai hito-desu-ne. (He is really great.)

and Mr. Takada agreed saying

Un, honto-ni rippa-dane. (Yes, it's really fine.)

Mr. Lerner remembered then that Miss Yoshida had laughed when he had once said *Rippana hi-desu-ne,* to mean "It's a fine day," shortly after joining the company.

* * *

Erai is used very commonly to praise someone's actions or behavior. The director of a company will show his appreciation of his men's hard work by saying

Erai. Yoku yatta.
えらい。よく やった。
(Good. You did a fine job.)

A mother will praise her child trying hard to help her, saying

Erai-wane. Doomo arigatoo.
(You're a good boy/girl. Thank you.)

As seen in the examples above, *erai* is used to praise the speaker's equals or younger people. You cannot directly say to a superior *Erai-desu-ne*.

The word *rippa* (fine) is used to praise a person's behavior or personality as in

> *Shachoo-wa rippana kata-desu. Sonna koto-wa kes-*
> 社長は　りっぱな　かたです。
> *shite nasaimasen.*

(The director is a person of fine character. He would never do such a thing.)

It is also used to praise man-made things. You can use it, for example, to refer to a stately building:

> *Rippana tatemono-desu.*
> りっぱな　建物です。
> (It's a magnificent building.)

But you cannot say things like *rippana tenki* (fine weather) or *rippana kawa* (a magnificent river). In this case you could say *ii tenki* or *ookina kawa*.

Okaimono-desu-ka
(Are you shopping?)

Last Saturday Mr. Lerner happened to meet Mrs. Takahashi, the wife of an acquaintance, at a department store. She bowed and said with a smile

Okaimono-desu-ka. (Are you shopping?)

Mr. Lerner knew that this is a set expression like *Odekake-desu-ka* used when meeting an acquaintance, but he wondered if he could also say *Kaimono-o shimasu-ka* (Do you buy things?) or *Okaimono-o nasaimasu-ka* (more polite).

      *   **   **

To make *dekakemasu-ka* more polite, you can use the *o . . . -ni narimasu-ka* pattern as in

Odekake-ni narimasu-ka.

In the same way, you can use the *. . .-o nasaru* pattern with *kaimono-o suru* as in

Kaimono-o nasaimasu-ka.

O can be added to make the expression even more polite:

Okaimono-o nasaimasu-ka.

Another polite form is *o . . . -desu-ka,* which can be used for *dekakemasu-ka* and *kaimono-o shimasu-ka.*

Odekake-desu-ka.
Okaimono-desu-ka.

This form sounds more indirect and therefore refined. Using verbs like *naru* or *nasaru* can sound rather direct, and *desu* is often preferred. Especially in set expressions like *odekake/okaimono-desu-ka*, this form is commonly used. To give several other examples of this type of expression:

> *Okaeri-desu-ka.*　お帰りですか。
> (Are you going home now?)
> *Oshigoto-desu-ka.*　お仕事ですか。
> (Are you working?)
> *Osanpo-desu-ka.*　お散歩ですか。
> (Are you taking a walk?)

This type of expression is actually used to express one's concern about the listener, rather than to ask for answers or information. *Odekake-desu-ka* often corresponds to "I see you're going out. Have a good time."

O . . . *-desu-ka* is also used for specific questions, usually with other phrases:

> *Nanji-goro okaeri-desu-ka.*
> (About what time are you/is he coming back?)
> *Kono waapuro, otsukai-desu-ka.*
> (Are you using this word processor?)

. . . *te-kuru* indicating the start of an action

Late yesterday afternoon when everyone was getting ready to leave the office, Miss Yoshida looked out the window, saying

A, tootoo futte-kimashita.
(Oh, it has finally started to rain.)

Mr. Lerner remembered that he had once said *furi-hajime-mashita* in a similar situation while Miss Yoshida said *furi-dashimashita*. Why do the Japanese use so many different expressions to refer to an action that's starting?

*   *   *

Among the several usages of . . . *te-kuru* is one indicating that an action has started:

Goji-goro-niwa kuraku natte-kuru.
暗く　なってくる
(It starts becoming dark around 5 o'clock.)
Densha-no mado-kara yama-ga miete-kita.
(We could start to see mountains through the windows of the train.)

This usage is similar to that indicating gradual change as in:

Samuku natte-kimashita-ne.
寒く　なってきましたね。
(It has become colder.)

In this case . . . *te-kuru* indicates a change that takes place over a period of time, but . . . *te-kuru* can also indicate a quick action as in *ame-ga futte-kita* 雨が　降ってきた .

To indicate the start of an action, -*hajimeru* and -*dasu* can also be used. *Hajimeru* is added to a verb when describing the start of an action as a fact, as in

Sanji-goro ame-ga furi-hajimeta.
(It started to rain at around 3.)

Dasu is added to a verb when the speaker describes the start of an action with some emotion like surprise, as in

A, ame-ga furi-dashita.
(Oh, it has started to rain.)
Aitsu kyuu-ni okori-dashita.
(He suddenly got angry.)

The expression . . . *te-kuru* is closer to -*dasu* than to -*hajimeru* in that it implies an emotional effect on the speaker. To compare the two, . . . *te-kuru* indicates a more direct effect than -*dasu*. Saying *ame-ga futte-kita* implies that the speaker is directly affected by the rainfall. It can imply things like "we will need umbrellas" or "we will have to give up going out."

. . . *dooshi* meaning 'keep . . .ing'

Yesterday morning Miss Yoshida reported that a co-worker, Mr. Kato, had become ill and been hospitalized. She said with a sigh

Tsukareta-n-desu-yo, kitto.
(He was very tired, I guess.)

and Mr. Takada agreed saying

Hataraki-dooshi-datta-kara-ne.
はたらきどおしだった

Mr. Lerner guessed that he meant that Mr. Kato had worked long hours, but the expression . . . *dooshi-datta* was new to him.

*   *   *

Dooshi is added to the stem of a verb as in

Hataraku — hataraki — hataraki-dooshi-da/desu

Hataraki-dooshi-da/desu means "he keeps working all the time." *Dooshi* can be added to various verbs as in

Tookyoo-kara Oosaka-made tachi-dooshi-datta.
立ちどおしだった
(I had to stand all the way from Tokyo to Osaka.)

Kaigi-no aida-juu inemuri-no shi-dooshi-nan-da-kara, komaru.
(He keeps sleeping all through the meeting. He really annoys me.)

You can also use . . . *tsuzukeru* to mean "keep

. . .ing'' as in

Asa-kara ban-made hataraki-tsuzukete-mo tsukare-masen.
(I can keep working from morning till night without getting tired.)

Dooshi differs from *tsuzukeru* in that it usually indicates a negative attitude toward the situation. *Dooshi* usually implies regret at having to keep doing something more than one wants to. *Tookyoo-kara Oosaka-made tachi-dooshi* implies that the speaker had to stand on the train when he wanted to have a seat. Conversely, if one said

Asa-kara ban-made suwari-dooshi-datta.
(I was sitting from morning till night.)

it implies that remaining seated for a long time made one tired.

Uses of *kekkoo* (good)

Miss Yoshida brought a cake she had made herself to the office yesterday. While eating it during the afternoon coffee break, Mr. Takada said

Kekkoo umai-ja nai-ka.

Mr. Lerner thought that he meant "It's very good, isn't it?," but Miss Yoshida did not thank him for the praise. As if to make up for Mr. Takada's remark, the other workers praised the cake lavishly. As a result, Mr. Lerner wondered what *kekkoo* means.

*   *   *

The word *kekkoo* has several usages. One means "good" as in

Kekkoona oaji-desu-ne.
けっこうな　お味ですね。
(It tastes very good.)
Sore-wa hontoo-ni kekkoo-desu-ne. (That is a very good idea.)

When used with a negative statement it means "not necessary."

A: *Moo sukoshi ikaga-desu-ka.*
(Would you like some more?)
B: *Iie, kekkoo-desu.*
いいえ、けっこうです。
(No, thank you.)

Kekkoo when used as an adverb means "unexpectedly" or "surprisingly." This was the *kekkoo* Mr. Takada used.

Kore, kekkoo oishii-desu-yo.
(This is better than you might think.)
Kore, kekkoo takakatta-n-desu-yo.
(This was surprisingly expensive.)
Kekkoo jikan-ga kakarimashita.
けっこう　時間が　かかりました。
(It took more time than I expected.)

Thus Mr. Takada's remark *kekkoo umai* was conditional praise. He implied that he had not expected her to be so good at making cakes. He probably chose this expression because he and Miss Yoshida are good friends; good friends often tease each other with this kind of reserved praise. A man will say to a good friend about his tennis or golf game

O, kekkoo yaru-ne.
(Oh, you are surprisingly good!)

Among the usages of *kekkoo,* the "good" and "not necessary" usage are appropriate in polite speech, but as an adverb it is used in familiar conversation.

Kotowaru meaning 'to give previous notice'

As the year end approaches Mr. Lerner's colleagues have started talking about having parties to forget the hardships of the past year. When Miss Yoshida mentioned a possible date, Mr. Takada agreed, and added

Demo, kotowatte-oku-kedo, kotoshi-wa nomenai-kara-ne.
(But I have to tell you that I cannot drink this year.)

Mr. Lerner knew that Mr. Takada, who was suffering from stomach trouble had to refrain from drinking, but he did not know the meaning of *koto-watte-oku*. Was he refusing to attend the party?

* * *

The verb *kotowaru* has several meanings. One of the most common is "to decline" or "to refuse" as in

Ano hanashi-wa kotowarimashita.
あの 話は ことわりました。
(I declined that offer.)
Tanonde-mita-kedo, kotowararete-shimatta.
(I asked him to do it, but he refused. — *lit.* I was refused.)

Another usage is "to tell someone beforehand" or "to give previous notice" as in

Tochuu-de heya-o deru toki-wa Yoshida-san-ni koto-watte-kudasai.
(When you're leaving the room before you're finished, please tell Miss Yoshida about it.)

104

As in Mr. Takada's sentence above, this usage of *kotowaru* is often joined with *oku* (do something beforehand), to make the meaning clearer. Mr. Takada meant by *kotowatte-oku* that he wants Miss Yoshida to understand and keep in mind that he cannot drink this year.

To give two more examples of *kotowatte-oku*:

Denwa-o kakete kotowatte-okeba, sukoshi-gurai okurete-mo daijoobu-desu.

電話を　かけて　ことわっておけば、少しぐらい おくれても　だいじょうぶです。

(If I telephone them beforehand, it will be all right to arrive a little late.)

Chotto okotowari-shite-okimasu-ga, kore-wa mada saishuu-kettee-ja arimasen-node, sono tsumori-de okiki-kudasai.

(I want to call your attention to the fact that this is not a final decision. Please listen to what I'm going to say with that in mind.)

Gakusee-ni suginai
(He's only a student)

During their coffee break yesterday, Mr. Lerner told Miss Yoshida about his trip to France several years before. When she asked him if he had dined at famous restaurants, Mr. Lerner said no, and added

Gakusee-dake-deshita-kara.

to mean "I was only a student." She understood but said *dake* was not necessary. Mr. Lerner wondered how the idea of "only" should be expressed in this case.

*   *   *

Nouns or pronouns with *dake* are used as in

Ato gofun-dake matte-kudasai.
(Please wait just 5 minutes more.)
Sonna koto-o ki-ni suru-nowa kimi-dake-dayo.
(No one else would be bothered by such a thing
— *lit.* You are the only person who is bothered by such a thing.)

When you want to describe a condition and emphasize its not amounting to much, *dake* is not used. Namely, you can say

Atsumatta-nowa gakusee-dake-datta.
あつまったのは　学生だけだった。
(Only students gathered.)

which actually means *Gakusee-dake-ga atsumatta*, but you cannot say

Kare-wa gakusee-dake-datta.

to mean "He was only a student." In the same way, you cannot say something like

Kore-wa joodan-dake-desu.

to mean "This is only a joke." In other words, where you would say in English "no more than . . . " you should avoid using "(pro)noun plus *dake*."

One way to express the idea of "no more than" is to use *ni suginai* as in

Tooji-wa gakusee-ni suginakatta.
当時は　学生に　すぎなかった。
(I was only a student then.)
Joodan-ni suginai koto-o ki-ni suru hitsuyoo-wa nai.
(One does not have to be bothered by a mere joke.)
Kore-wa watashi-no kojintekina iken-ni sugimasen-ga . . .
(This is nothing more than my personal opinion.)

The *ni suginai* form, however, is used in formal speech or written language. In conversation, other expressions like *mada* ([not] yet) and *honno* (only/mere) are used before nouns:

Sono koro-wa mada gakusee-deshita-kara.
その　ころは　まだ　学生でしたから。
(I was still only a student then.)
Honno joodan-desu-yo.
(It's just a joke.)

107

. . . mo aru-shi, . . . mo aru
(There are . . . and . . .)

Miss Yoshida was looking sad over a mistake she had made as she was leaving the office. Mr. Takada noticed and told her not to take it so hard, whatever it might be, and added

Ii koto-mo aru-shi, warui koto-mo aru-yo.
(There are good things as well as bad things.)

Mr. Lerner thought that *. . . shi* is used to connect two similar statements; he did not know that it can also be used to connect two opposite statements.

* * *

. . . shi is usually used to connect similar statements, as in

Samui-shi, ame-mo futte-iru.
(It's cold and raining.)
Ano-hito-wa atama-mo ii-shi, karada-mo joobu-da.
あの人は　頭も　いいし、体も　じょうぶだ。
(He is both bright and healthy.)

It is used to connect two or more statements which serve the same purpose. In the first example above, *shi* is connecting two statements about bad weather, and in the second two good points of a person are stated with *shi*.

In Mr. Takada's sentence above, *ii koto-mo aru* and *warui koto-mo aru* seem to be quite different from each other, but they serve the same purpose: In this case, the two statements are used to describe how the world is. He meant that the world is not always bad, and one should not be discouraged easily. The same idea is idiomatically expressed as

108

Teru hi-mo aru-shi, kumoru hi-mo aru.
照る　日も　あるし、くもる　日も　ある。
(There are fair days and cloudy days.)

A similar expression . . . *tari* is also used to connect two opposite-sounding statements to describe a certain condition:

Ureshii koto-ga attari, iyana koto-ga attari suru.
(There are happy experiences as well as unpleasant ones.)
Kono-goro-wa samukattari atsukattari suru.
(It is sometimes cold and sometimes hot these days.)

Ima hitotsu meaning
'something more is needed'

Miss Yoshida brought several paintings that she had made to the office and asked Mr. Takada his opinion of them. Mr. Takada praised one of them lavishly, but when he picked up another he said:

Kotchi-wa ima hitotsu-dane.

Mr. Lerner did not understand this expression. But seeing the way Miss Yoshida reacted to the comment, he imagined the *ima hitotsu* means "not very good."

* * *

The word *ima* (now) means "more" when it precedes a word indicating amount or time:

Ima sukoshi yasukereba kau-n-desu-kedo.
(If it were a little cheaper, I would buy it.)
Ima shibaraku omachi-kudasai.
いま　しばらく　お待ちください。
(Please wait a little longer.)

In such expressions *ima* is used as a synonym of *moo*. Thus, *ima hitotsu* literally means "one more" as in:

Sono okashi ima hitotsu kurenai?
(Please give me one more of the candies.)

But when it is used in *ima hitotsu-da*, it indicates the speaker's judgment that something should be a little better. When Mr. Takada used it in his evaluation of Miss Yoshida's painting, he meant that somehow something is missing to make it really

110

attractive. *Ima hitotsu-da* is used for evaluation as in:

> *Daitai ii-n-da-kedo, ima hitotsu-dane.*
> だいたい　いいんだけど、いま　ひとつだね。
> (It's almost right but lacks something.)
> *Ano otoko, shigoto-wa dekiru-n-da-kedo, taido-ga ima hitotsu-na-n-dene . . .*
> (He is capable, but I don't much like his attitude.)

Recently, young people tend to use *ima ichi*, replacing *hitotsu* (a piece) with *ichi* (number one):

> A: *Kore doo?*
> (How about this?)
> B: *Uun, ima ichi-jan?*
> (Well, it's not quite right, don't you think?)

Both *ima hitotsu* and *ima ichi* are conversational, but the latter sounds definitely familiar.

Apologies and the use of *kara*

Mr. Lerner wanted to ask Miss Yoshida a few questions about his work. Although she seemed busy, he approached her because his questions were rather urgent. He started by saying:

Ojama-desu-kara sumimasen.

meaning "I'm sorry to disturb you." She kindly answered all his questions, but after that she said *ojama-desu-kara* should be replaced by *ojama-shite.* Mr. Lerner had noticed that the Japanese often use . . . *kara* when making a request, and so he had used it. But *kara* is inappropriate for offering an apology.

*　　　*　　　*

It is true that *kara* is often used in requests and offers when an English-speaker would not use any conjunction at all:

Moo sugu owarimasu-kara chotto matte-ite-kudasai.
(I'm going to be finished soon. Could you wait a little bit?)
Shokuji-no shitaku-ga demimashita-kara doozo.
(The meal is ready. Please come and eat.)

In these examples, phrases ending in *kara* are used to indicate a situation that is felt to be appropriate for making a request. Namely, the work being almost completed encourages the speaker to dare ask someone to wait; the meal being ready causes the speaker to invite someone to come and eat.

But phrases ending in *kara* are not used when offering an apology; *ojama-desu-kara* cannot be followed by *sumimasen* (I'm sorry). An apology should be preceded by . . . *te* (. . . *ing*) rather than . . . *kara* (because).

> *Ojikan-o torimashite mooshiwake arimasen.*
> お時間を とりまして 申しわけ ありません。
> (I'm very sorry to have taken your time.)
> *Osoku natte gomen-nasai.*
> おそく なって ごめんなさい。
> (Sorry I'm late.)

Recently the authors received a letter from abroad saying:

> *Totsuzen-no tegami-desu-kara mooshiwake arimasen.*

This should be corrected to:

> *Totsuzen otegami-o sashiagemashite, mooshiwake arimasen.*
> (I'm sorry to be writing to you so, abruptly.)

The differences between *wa* and *mo*

At lunchtime yesterday Mr. Lerner was talking about traveling with several colleagues. He said:

Amerika-ni ita toki-wa yoku ryokoo-shimashita.
(When I was living in the United States, I used to travel a lot.)

Then Miss Yoshida said:

Nihon-dewa amari shinai-n-desu-ka.
(You don't travel much in Japan, do you?)

Actually, Mr. Lerner was going to say that he travels a lot in Japan too. He wondered why she anticipated that he was going to say he didn't.

* * *

Miss Yoshida expected Mr. Lerner to say that he does not travel much in Japan because he said, *Amerika-ni ita toki-wa . . .* The particle *wa* usually suggests a contrasting or opposing statement in what follows. If Mr. Lerner had said:

Amerika-ni ita toki-mo . . .

she would have expected him to say that he traveled a lot in Japan too.

In the same way, if someone has said:

Ocha-wa suki-da-kedo . . .
お茶は　すきだけど……
(I like tea but . . .)

114

the listener will expect him to say something like:

Koohii-wa kirai-desu. (I don't like coffee.)
or
Kyoo-wa koohii-ni shiyoo.
(I think I'll have coffee today.)

If the speaker has said:

Ocha-mo suki-da-kedo . . .
お茶も　すきだけど……

the listener will expect him to say something like:

Koohii-mo kirai-ja nai. (I don't dislike coffee.)

A native speaker of a language can easily anticipate what follows or what is likely to follow, and this makes listening comprehension easy, while a foreigner often has to listen attentively to understand what has been said. Also, when a foreigner speaks in a way that is contrary to a native listener's anticipation, the listener finds it hard to listen to him. The use of *mo* and *wa* is one of the factors that helps a listener anticipate what is likely to follow.

Expressions meaning 'I think that . . .'

At lunchtime yesterday the people at work started discussing professional baseball. When someone mentioned a player and said that he had improved a lot recently, Mr. Lerner agreed, saying,

Ee, boku-mo soo-to omoimasu.

meaning "Yes, I think so, too." Later Miss Yoshida said that *to* should be left out in *soo-to omoimasu.* Mr. Lerner remembered that he had once been told that, but he still tends to say *to* whenever *omoimasu* follows.

* * *

To mean "I think that . . .," usually *. . . to omou/omoimasu* is used as in:

Watashi-wa kono hoo-ga ii-to omoimasu.
(I think this is better.)
Boku, ano-hito kuru-to omou-yo.
(I think she will come.)
Are-wa dame-da-to omou.
(I think that is not OK.)

But when *omoimasu* follows *soo* (that way), *koo* (this way), and *doo* (how/what), *to* is not used.

Watashi-wa koo omoimasu.
わたしは　こう　思います。
(This is what I think.)
Kore, doo omoimasu-ka.
(What do you think of this?)

When *da* is added to the words above, *to omo-*

116

imasu is used:

> *Soo-da-to omoimasu.*
> そうだと　思います。
> (I think that is so.)

Thus, *soo omoimasu* and *soo-da-to omoimasu* are correct while *soo-to omoimasu* sounds strange.

The negation *nai* is also followed by *to omou* as in:

> *Soo-ja nai-to omou.*
> そうじゃ　ないと　思う。
> (I don't think so.)
> *Ano-hito-wa konai-to omoimasu.*
> (I don't think he will come.)

Saying,

> *Soo-da-to omoimasen.*
> *Ano-hito-wa kuru-to omoimasen.*

is possible, but is not common; it is used only when "I don't think" is to be emphasized.

Sanji-ni (at three) and *sanji-kara* (from three)

Mr. Lerner asked Miss Yoshida what time the next meeting would start. She answered:

Kin'yoobi-no sanji-kara-desu-yo.
(It will be from three on Friday.)

It was a very simple exchange, but he suddenly realized that the Japanese often say . . . *kara-desu* instead of . . . *ni hajimarimasu.*

*　　*　　*

To mean "It starts at three," you can say either:

Sanji-ni hajimarimasu.
三時に　はじまります。

or

Sanji-kara hajimarimasu.
三時から　はじまります。

The second phrase is often simplified to:

Sanji-kara-desu.
三時からです。

. . . *ni*, as in *sanji-ni*, is used when the speaker's interest is in what time something starts, while *kara*, as in *sanji-kara*, is used when he wants to emphasize that the action will start at a certain time and keep going for some time.

Actually . . . *kara* very often used with *hajimaru* and *hajimeru* (to start doing something) as in:

Kaigi-wa sanji-kara hajimarimasu.
(The meeting starts at three.)

118

This is why a Japanese student of English tends to say "School starts from nine" when he should say "School starts at nine."

When continued action is implied, *kara* is used without a verb meaning "to start." ✓

Ashita-kara hayaku okiru.
あしたから　早く　おきる。

means "I will start getting up early from tomorrow." In the same way,

Rainen-kara sake-o yameru.

means "I will stop drinking next year and will not drink after that."

This usage of *kara* is seen in talking about space, too:

Doko-kara sooji-shimashoo-ka.
(What place shall I clean first?)
Mondai-ga ookisugite, doko-kara te-o tsukereba ii-ka wakaranai.

(The problem is so big I don't know where to start in solving it.)

Dareka inai-ka-to omotte . . .
(wondering if there isn't someone . . .)

A few days ago Miss Yoshida showed Mr. Lerner a concert ticket for the following day and explained that she could not go and wanted to find someone to go in her place. She used the phrase,

Dareka ikeru hito-ga inai-ka-to omotte . . .
だれか　行ける　人が　いないかと　思って……

meaning, "I brought this ticket wondering if there wasn't someone who could use it." Mr. Lerner understood but wondered if she could also have said:

Dareka . . . iru-ka-to omotte . . .

*　　*　　*

Miss Yoshida could also have said:

Dareka ikeru hito-ga iru-ka-to omotte . . .

But the *inai* expression is more common in this situation.

When the speaker is interested simply in knowing whether there is someone who can go, *ikeru hito-ga iru-ka-to omotte . . .* is more common. On the other hand, when the speaker expects or wishes to find someone, *inai,* the negative expression, is more commonly used.

Similarly, a newscaster will say something like:

. . . mokugekisha-ga inai-ka dooka shirabete-imasu.
……目撃者がいないか　どうか　調べています。
(. . . they are trying to find out if there were any eyewitnesses.)

One could also say,

. . . *mokugekisha-ga iru-ka dooka* . . .

but when a witness is wanted by the police, . . . *inai-ka* is more commonly used.

When a hungry husband is looking inside the refrigerator, and his wife questions him about what he is doing, he is more likely to say:

Nanika taberu mono-ga nai-ka-to omotte sagashite-iru-n-da.

(I'm looking to see if there is something to eat.)

Not only in the case of an inquiry into the existence of something, but also in the case of expressing a wish, *nai* is usually used:

Aa, nanika ii koto nai-ka-naa.
ああ、何か いい こと ないかなあ。

(Oh, I wish I could come across something nice.)

Nanishiro used for emphasis

Yesterday afternoon Mr. Okada came to have a business discussion with Mr. Lerner and Mr. Takada. He had first planned to come a week earlier, but had postponed by a week. Before starting he apologized for changing the date and added:

Nanishiro isogashikatta-node . . .
なにしろ　いそがしかったので……

Mr. Lerner understood that he had been busy, but he did not know the meaning of the word *nanishiro,* which he imagined to mean "very much."

           *   *   *

Nanishiro literally means "whatever it may be" and is actually used to emphasize what the speaker wants to say:

Nanishiro mono-ga takaku narimashita-kara-ne . . .
(Things have really become expensive.)
Ano-hito-wa nanishiro kattena koto-o yuu mono-de . . .
(Since he wants to force his way. . . .)

It resembles *tonikaku* (at any rate, whatever it may be), and *tonikaku* can replace *nanishiro* in Mr. Okada's speech and the two sentences above. However there is a difference between the two: *tonikaku* is also used when the speaker proposes an action or requests the listener to do something.

Dekiru-ka dooka tonikaku yatte-mimashoo.
　　　　　　とにかく　やってみましよう
(At any rate, I will do whatever I can.)

Tonikaku yatte-mite-kudasai.
(Please give it a try, anyway.)

But in these two examples *nanishiro* cannot replace *tonikaku*.

Nanishiro is most often used to invite the listener's agreement or to give an excuse by emphatically stating the speaker's judgment:

Nanishiro zairyoo-ga takai-node, yasuku dekinai-n-desu.
(Since the raw materials are so expensive, we can't sell them any cheaper.)

Odorokimashita-nee. Nanishiro ano-hito-ga anna koto-o shita-n-desu-kara.
(It was so surprising, wasn't it? No one ever expected him to do such a thing.)

Nandaka preceding the expression of feeling

Mr. Lerner ran into Miss Yoshida on the way to the office yesterday morning. It was a sunny day, and she said,

> *Nandaka ii koto-ga aru-yoona ki-ga shimasu.*
> なんだか いい ことが あるような 気が します。
> (Somehow I feel like something nice will happen.)

He understood her but did not exactly understand the meaning of *nandaka*.

* * *

Nandaka literally means "what it is." It is used in that sense in a sentence like:

> *Nan-da-ka wakarimasen. Akete-mimashoo.*
> (I don't know what it is. I'll open it and find out.)

But in a sentence like Miss Yoshida's, *nandaka* is used to mean "somehow — although what it is is not known." This is used before an expression of feeling as in:

> *Kyoo-wa nandaka ureshii.*
> (For some reason or other I feel happy today.)
> *Ano-hito nandaka ki-ni iranai.*
> あの人 なんだか 気に いらない。
> (Somehow I don't like him.)
> *Nandaka ikitaku nai-kedo, shikata-ga nai-kara iku.*
> (I don't feel like going, but I'm going to go because I have to.)

Nandaka is often followed by . . . *ki-ga suru,* which means "I feel that . . ./I have a hunch that . . ." as in Miss Yoshida's statement above.

> *Nandaka umaku ikisoona ki-ga shimasu-yo.*
> (I have a hunch that it will go well.)
> *Ee, nandaka sonna ki-ga shimasu-ne.*
> (Yes, I have that feeling, too.)

Nan-to naku (for no particular reason) is used in a very similar way. It can replace *nandaka* in the examples above. The difference is that *nan-to naku* sounds more refined and formal; it can be used in polite speech and in letters, but *nandaka* is limited to familiar conversations.

Tema (one's time/labor)

Yesterday afternoon a man came to the office to see Mr. Lerner with a letter of introduction from Mr. Okada, an acquaintance of Mr. Lerner. The man said he wanted Mr. Lerner's advice on a project of his. Before starting his explanation of the project, he asked Mr. Lerner's permission, saying,

> *Otema-wa torasemasen-kara.*
> お手間は　とらせませんから。

Although Mr. Lerner did not understand this expression he imagined that it meant that the explanation wouldn't take long.

*　　　*　　　*

The word *tema* means "time" or "labor" as in:

> *Kono shigoto-wa tema-ga kakaru.*
> (This work requires a lot of time.)
> *Chotto junbi-ni tema-o totta.*
> (It took some time to prepare for it.)

Tema is used with the verbs *kakaru* and *toru,* both of which mean "to take." *Otema-o toraseru* literally means "to cause it to take your time." *Otema-wa torasemasen* means "It will not take too much of your time." This phrase is often used to ask someone politely if he would spare some time:

> *Otema-wa torasemasen-kara, chotto ohairi-kudasai-masen-ka.*
> (Would you kindly come in? It won't take much time.)

Tema-o toru is often pronounced as *tema-doru,* and

126

this phrase is used to mean "time-taking":

Osoi-naa. Nan-ni tema-dotte-iru-n-daroo.
おそいなあ。何に　手間どっているんだろう。
(He is so late. I wonder what's keeping him.)

Tesuu is also used to mean "time" or "labor/trouble."

Otesuu-o kakete sumimasen.
お手数を　かけて　すみません。
(I'm sorry I took your time.)
Kono shigoto-wa tesuu-ga kakaru.
(This work requires a lot of time.)

The two are often interchangeable, but *tesuu* emphasizes one's labor or trouble, while *tema* emphasizes the amount of time spent on the work.

Both *tema* and *tesuu* refer to a human being's time, while *jikan* refers to time in general. You can say,

Ojikan-wa kakarimasen-kara.

in the same meaning as *Otema-wa torasemasen-kara,* but you cannot say something like:

Mada tema/tesuu-ga juubun nokotte-iru.
(We have plenty of time yet.)

127

Expressions indicating the cause of emotion

Mr. Kobayashi, the youngest worker in the office, suddenly exclaimed out loud when he was reading the newspaper yesterday morning. He said he had won a large amount of money in the lottery. While he was talking happily, Mr. Kato came into the room and asked,

Nani-o sonna-ni yorokonde-iru-n-da.
何を そんなに よろこんでいるんだ。
(What are you so happy about?)

Mr. Lerner did not know that *o* could be used to indicate the cause of joy.

* * *

Adjectives expressing emotions are usually followed by *ga*:

Nani-ga sonna-ni ureshii-no.
何が そんなに うれしいの。
(What are you so happy about?)
Tomodachi-ga natsukashii.
(I miss my friends.)
Kinoo-no shippai-ga zannen-da.
(I regret the mistake I made yesterday.)

When these adjectives are changed into verbs by replacing the last *i* with *garu* as in *ureshii* — *ureshigaru, natsukashii* — *natsukashigaru*, they are followed by *o*:

Kodomo-wa koinu-ga shinda-no-o kanashigatte, go-han-mo tabenai.
(The child is so sad about the puppy's death that she won't eat.)

128

Shachoo, ano koto-o zannengatte-ita-yo.
社長、あの ことを 残念がっていたよ。
(**The firm's director** was very sorry about that.)

Some other verbs expressing emotion are also used with *o* — *yorokobu, kanashimu* (be sad about), and *okoru* (be angry) are used with *o*:

Kare, mada boku-no koto-o okotte-iru-rashii.
(He seems to still be angry with me.)

Other verbs are used with *o*, *ni* or . . .*no koto-de*, depending on the situation or the style of speech. When they are used in questions starting with *nani*, they are used with *o*.

Kare, nani-o nayande-iru-n-deshoo.
(I wonder what he is worrying about.)
Monooto-ni odoroite, kinjo-no hito-ga atsumatte-kita.
(The neighbors came out when they heard the noise — *lit*. The neighbors were surprised by the noise and gathered together.)
Kanojo-no koto-de nayande-iru-n-da-yo, kitto.
(I bet he's worrying about his girlfriend.)

Kurushii and *tsurai* (painful)

Mr. Okada was very busy after being promoted to section chief and had not come to see Mr. Lerner for a month. When he finally came by yesterday, Mr. Lerner congratulated him on his promotion, but he responded,

Iya, tsurai mon-desu-ne, choo-ni naru-nowa.
(Well, it's hard becoming a chief.)

Mr. Lerner imagined that meant that it was tough to be in an administrative position, but he was not sure about the exact meaning of the word *tsurai*. Was it a synonym for *kurushii*?

*   *   *

People often complain about their suffering using *kurushii* or *tsurai*. The two seem to be close in meaning, and sometimes can be used in the same situation, but there is some difference between them.

Kurushii is used to refer to direct physical pain or suffering as in:

Kaze-de hana-ga tsumatte kurushii.
(I have a cold, and my nose is stuffed up. I'm suffering.)

Takai yama-no ue-wa kuuki-ga usui-kara kokyuu-ga
空気が　うすいから　呼吸が
kurushii.
くるしい

(The air near a high mountain's peak is thin so it is hard to breathe.)

Tsurai is commonly used to refer to psychological pain caused by physical pain:

130

Koshi-ga itakute tsurai.
(My lower back hurts; it's very trying.)

Both *kurushii* and *tsurai* are used for nonphysical pain, too, but *kurushii* is more commonly used for economic hardship:

Kodomo-ga ooi-kara ima-no gekkyuu-dewa kurushii.
子どもが 多いから いまの 月給では くるしい。
(It is difficult to survive on my present pay with my many children.)

On the other hand, *tsurai* is commonly used to refer to one's emotional difficulty in terms of human relationships:

Anna ii hito-ni uso-o tsuku-nowa tsurai.
あんな いい 人に うそを つくのは つらい。
(It's painful to tell a lie to such a good person.)
Toshi-o toru-to hito-ni tsukawareru-noga tsuraku naru.
(When one becomes older, it becomes hard to work under someone else.)

Mr. Okada used *tsurai* in this sense; probably it is painful for him to act as a boss over his former colleagues.

. . . *dano* . . . *dano* (. . . and . . .)

Miss Yoshida was reading a newspaper at lunchtime yesterday. Mr. Takada passed by her, asking if there was anything interesting. She answered no, and added,

Satsujin-dano yuukai-dano, kurai nyuusu-bakari-desu.
(Murder, kidnapping . . . nothing but gloomy news.)

Mr. Lerner imagined that *dano* meant "and" like *ya* or *toka,* but this *dano* was new to him.

* * *

Various expressions are used when citing two or more things as examples. *Ya* is used to name two or more things, implying that the speaker has not named everything:

Yamada-san-ya Tanaka-san-ga kimashita.
山田さんや　田中さんが　来ました。
(Mr. Yamada and Mr. Tanaka came.)

implies that other people came too. *To* is used to imply that every name has been given:

Yamada-san-to Tanaka-san-ga kimashita.
山田さんと　田中さんが　来ました。
(Mr. Yamada and Mr. Tanaka came.)

means just the two of them came.

While *ya* is used both in conversation and written language, *toka* and *dano* are used only in conversation. To compare the two, *dano* is used mainly

132

with a negative implication while *toka* is used either positively or negatively.

Ano-hito, ocha-toka ohana-toka iroiro naratte-iru.
(She is studying various things, such as tea ceremony and flower arrangement.)

Ocha-toka ohana-toka moo furui-yo.
お茶とか　お花とか　もう　古いよ。
(The tea ceremony and flower arrangement are so old-fashioned!)

Ocha-dano ohana-dano, yaritaku nai-wa.
お茶だの　お花だの、やりたく　ないわ。
(I don't care for the tea ceremony or flower arrangement.)

Miss Yoshida used *dano* when mentioning murder and kidnapping; she could have used *toka* instead, but *dano* more clearly reflected her unpleasant feelings about the news.

Toka and *dano* are different from *ya* in that they can also be used to connect quoted statements:

Shigoto-ga ooi-dano yasumi-ga sukunai-dano, monku-bakari itte-iru.
仕事が　多いだの　休みが　少ないだの、文句ばかり　言っている。
(He is always complaining that he has to work a lot or that he doesn't have enough time off.)

Amari . . . nai (not . . . much) (2)

Mr. Lerner, Mr. Takada and Miss Yoshida went to a coffee shop near the office for a cup of coffee after lunch yesterday. Mr. Takada asked Mr. Lerner,

Koko-ewa yoku kimasu-ka.
(Do you often come here?)

and he answered,

Iie, yoku kimasen.
(No, I don't come often.)

Then Miss Yoshida said *yoku kimasen* sounded a little odd to her.

*   *   *

Yoku is used in several different meanings. One is to express "often" or "much":

Gakusee-no koro-wa yoku eega-o mimashita.
(I often went to see movies when I was a student.)
Kinoo-wa yoku furimashita-ne.
きのうは　よく　降りましたね。
(It rained a lot yesterday.)

The opposite of *yoku* in this sense is usually *amari*:

Gakusee-no koro-wa amari eega-wa mimasen-de-shita.
(I didn't go to the movies very often when I was a student.)
Kinoo-wa amari furimasen-deshita-ne.
きのうは　あまり　降りませんでしたね。

(It didn't rain much yesterday.)

Saying *yoku kimasen* can be understood but sounds strange, since with *yoku* one usually expects an affirmative ending to the sentence.

But when *yoku* is used in the sense of "well" or "skillfully," it is often followed by the negative:

Furansugo-wa yoku wakarimasen.
フランス語は　よく　わかりません。
(I don't know French very well.)
Yoku dekimasen-kedo, yatte-mimasu.
(I can't do it very well, but I'll try.)

But when *yoku* is used in the sense of "often" or "much," *amari* is more appropriate with the negative.

In Japanese the first part of a sentence often indicates that the end of the sentence will be in the negative. When one has heard,

Kinoo-wa amari furi . . .

or

Gakusee-no koro-wa amari eega-wa mi . . .

one expects the ending to be in the negative. Thus the last part of a sentence can often be left out as it is understood. In reply to Mr. Takada's question, *Koko-ewa yoku kimasu-ka,* Mr. Lerner could have just said,

Iie, amari . . .
(No, not very often.)

Nuances of . . .*n-da-kara*

Mr. Lerner was planning to leave the office early yesterday and told Miss Yoshida, adding,

Yooji-ga aru-n-da-kara.
(Since I have something to do . . .)

She smiled as if to remind him of his inappropriate wording. Mr. Lerner did not understand what she was hinting at, and she explained that he had used, as he often did, . . .*n-da-kara* in an aggressive-sounding way.

* * *

Mr. Lerner should have said,

Yooji-ga aru-node. 用事が あるので。

or

Yooji-ga arimasu-kara.

rather than *Yooji-ga aru-n-da-kara* 用事が あるんだから .

. . .*n-desu/da-kara* is used to explain emphatically a situation. It is often used to give a reason for one's feelings:

Nan-demo agaru-n-da-kara iya-ni narimasu-ne.
(It's annoying how everything keeps getting more expensive.)
Kono kaze, chittomo naoranai-n-da-kara, komat-chau.
(I just can't get rid of my cold no matter what I do!)

When it is used to give a reason for one's actions, it often sounds self-defensive. Saying,

Yooji-ga aru-n-da-kara hayaku kaerimasu.
(Since I have something to do, I'm leaving early.)

sounds as if one is saying "What's wrong with my leaving early? I have a reason — I have something to do."

In the same way, saying,

Kaze-o hiite-iru-n-desu-kara, yasumimasu.
(Since I have a cold, I won't be coming to the office.)

implies, "You shouldn't complain about my being absent."

In short, using . . .*n-desu/da-kara* instead of . . .*desu/da-kara* often presupposes the listener's disagreement or disapproval. Therefore it sounds overly defensive when used to explain one's own actions. It can be used, however, when you want to overcome a listener's reserve about accepting your offer.

Boku-ga sasotta-n-desu-kara, harawasete-kudasai-yo.
(I insist that I pay, since I asked you.)
Oisogashii-n-desu-kara, watashi-no hoo-kara ukagaimasu.
(Since you are so busy, I will come to see you [rather than having you come to me].)

. . . *eba* used for giving advice

When Mr. Lerner walked by Mr. Kobayashi and Miss Yoshida talking in the hall yesterday, he heard her say,

Ja, soo sureba.
じゃ、そう　すれば。

(Then why don't you do so?)

Mr. Lerner understood that she was giving a piece of advice, but he did not know that . . . *eba* could be used for giving advice; he had thought . . . *tara* is used for this purpose.

* * *

. . . *tara doo-desu-ka* is commonly used when offering advice; *ikaga* is used instead of *doo* to be polite, and *doo* alone is used in familiar speech. In familiar speech, *doo* is often left out, and just . . . *tara* is used for giving advice.

Moo sorosoro kaettara.
もう　そろそろ　帰ったら。

(You can leave now, if you'd like.)
Ja, soo shitara.
(Why don't you do so?)

On the other hand, . . .*eba* as in *sureba* (if you do) or *ikeba* (if you go) is not commonly followed by *doo-desu-ka* or *doo*. It is commonly followed by *ii* (all right / good) giving permission:

Ashita sureba ii.
(You can do it tomorrow. — *lit.* If you do it tomorrow, it will be all right.)

138

Ato-de ikeba ii-desu-yo.

(You can go later. — implying "you don't have to go now.")

Saying just . . . *eba* is not used for giving advice as commonly as . . . *tara*. When advice is given in the form of . . . *eba*, it indicates a detached attitude rather than enthusiasm toward helping the listener. Saying *ikeba*, for instance, implies, "You can go since it is what you think is best. I don't care what you do." It often indicates a lack of interest:

A: *Ashita-ni shitara.*
   (Why don't you do it tomorrow?)
B: *Un, demo kyoo yaritai-n-da.*
   (Well, I really want to do it today.)
A: *Aa, soo. Ja, soo sureba.*
   (Oh? Why don't you go ahead and do it then?)

Soo omoimasu (I think so)

Miss Yoshida said that it was time to start planning for *gooruden wiiku* (Golden Week — the consecutive holidays from the end of April to the beginning of May). Mr. Lerner agreed,

> *Ee, soo-to omoimasu.*

meaning, "Yes, I think so." She smiled and said that he had made the old mistake again before he corrected himself,

> *Ee, soo omoimasu.*
> ええ、そう　思います。

* * *

It is a common mistake to say *Soo-to omoimasu* for *Soo omoimasu*. The expression *omoimasu* (I think) is usually preceded by *to*:

> *Ano-hito-wa kuru-to omoimasu.*
> (I think he will come.)
> *Kore-wa ii shina-da-to omoimasu.*
> (I think this is a fine piece of merchandise.)

But *soo* (that way) is an adverb used directly before a verb or adjective:

> *Soo shimashoo.*
> そう　しましょう。
> (Let's do that.)
> *Soo takaku-wa arimasen.*
> (It's not that expensive.)

Therefore *soo* is directly followed by *omoimasu* without *to*.

Koo (this way), *aa* (that way) and *doo* (in what way) are also used as adverbs:

Koo sureba hayaku dekimasu.
こう すれば 早く できます。
(You can do it quickly if you do it this way.)
Aa ganko-dewa hito-ni kirawareru-daroo.
(Since he is that stubborn he will be disliked by others.)
Doo ikeba ii-deshoo?
(How should I go there?)

You can also say

Soo-da-to omoimasu.
(I think that it is so.)

since *soo-da* means "it is so."

All in all, you can say either *Soo omoimasu* or *Soo-da-to omoimasu*, but not *Soo-to omoimasu*. The difference between *Soo omoimasu* and *Soo-da-to omoimasu* is rather small; the latter sounds more definite.

...*te* meaning 'a person who...'

The other day Mr. Takada asked Mr. Kobayashi, the youngest worker in the company, when he would be getting married. Mr. Kobayashi laughed and said,

Kite-ga arimasen-kara.

Mr. Lerner did not know the word *kite*, although he imagined that Mr. Kobayashi was saying that he had not found anyone to marry yet.

*   *   *

The word *te*, which by itself means "hand," is used to mean "a person who does something" or "an agent." The word *kite* is a combination of *ki*, the stem of *kuru* (to come) and this *te*. This means "someone who will come" (usually to get married or to be employed). Mr. Kobayashi meant that nobody is willing to come to marry him. Similarly, a director of a small company may say something like:

Uchi-no yoona chiisai kaisha-niwa nakanaka kite-ga nai.

(It is difficult to find workers to join a small company like ours.)

Te is added to the stem of basic action verbs:

hanasu (speak) — *hanashite* 話し手 (speaker)
kiku (listen) — *kikite* 聞き手 (listener)
kau (buy) — *kaite* 買い手 (buyer)
uru (sell) — *urite* 売り手 (seller)

They might be used in the following ways:

142

Kikite-ni yoku wakaru yoo-ni hanasanakute-wa ike-nai.

(You should speak in a way that a listener can easily understand you.)

Sonna nedan-dewa kaite-ga tsukanai-daroo.

(No one will buy it at such a price.)

Te is added mostly to the stem of verbs indicating a physical, rather than mental or psychological, action. You cannot say something like *wakari-te* (a person who understands) or *kangae-te* (a person who thinks). And *te* is most commonly added to verbs referring to actions that affect someone else, as in *kaite* (buyer) and *urite* (seller). One does not say *hashirite* (runner) to refer to a person who is hurrying to the station, but this can be used in a running race, as runners have definite roles in the race. You don't refer to a customer in a restaurant as *tabete* (an eater), though you can say something like:

Kono keeki, amaku shisugita-node, tabete-ga inai.

(I made this cake too sweet, so nobody will eat it.)

143

Ichido and *ikkai* (one time)

A Mr. Kondo came to see Mr. Lerner the other day through the introduction of a friend. When their discussion was over, and Mr. Kondo was leaving, he said,

Doozo watashidomo-no kaisha-emo oide-kudasai.
(Please visit us at our company.)

So Mr. Lerner answered,

Hai, ikkai ukagaimasu.

to mean "Yes, I will come some time." Miss Yoshida, who was with them, said *ikkai* cannot be used in place of *ichido* in that situation, although both mean "one time."

*　　　*　　　*

Both *do* and *kai* are used to refer to frequency, as in:

one time —*ichido/ikkai*
two times —*nido/nikai*
three times —*sando/sankai*
ten times —*juudo/jikkai*

You can say either,

Asoko-e sando ikimashita.
(I went there three times.)
or
Asoko-e sankai ikimashita.
(I went there three times.)

When referring purely to frequency, both *do* and *kai*

144

are used with no difference in meaning.

But when "one time" is used to mean "sometime in the future," *ichido* must be used:

> *Ichido ome-ni kakaritai-to omoimasu.*
> 一度　お目に　かかりたいと　思います。
> (I'd like to see you sometime.)

In this usage, *ichido* does not mean "once, not twice"; it simply refers to some indefinite future occurrence. In this sense it resembles such expressions as:

> *Hitotsu meshiagatte-kudasai.*
> (Please have some.)

Kai is used in factual reports; in scientific writing or when referring to large numbers, *kai* rather than *do* is used.

> *Juunen-kan-ni sanjuu-go-kai sono kuni-o otozureta.*
> 十年間に　三十五回　その　国を　おとずれた。
> (He visited the country 35 times in 10 years.)

Yoru (draw near)

At lunchtime yesterday Mr. Lerner was taking a walk in the park near the office when he saw a group of young workers standing in front of a man with a camera. The man said to them,

Motto yotte, yotte.

From the way the man moved his hand Mr. Lerner understood that he wanted them to come closer to each other, but he did not know the word *yotte*.

* * *

Yotte is the *te* form of the verb *yoru* (draw nearer, approach) and is used to convey a command. The *te* form is often used in familiar speech in place of . . . *te-kudasai* (please . . .).

The verb *yoru* is used in various ways. It is used in the sense of "draw nearer, approach":

Moo sukoshi kotchi-ni yoreba moo hitori kakerare-masu-yo.

(If you move over toward me a little more, one more person can sit down here.)

Abunai-kara yoranaide-kudasai.
あぶないから　寄らないでください。

(Please don't go any closer. It's dangerous.)

The stem *yori* is often added to nouns:

Shinjuku-yori-no kaidan-o orita hoo-ga ii.
新宿寄りの　階段

(You/we should go down the stairs in the direction of Shinjuku [on a train platform.])

Ano seejika, mushozoku-da-kedo, jimintoo-yori-rashii.

(That politician belongs to no party, but he seems to lean toward the Liberal-Democratic Party.)

Yoru is often used when one asks someone to drop in at one's home.

Chotto yotte-ikimasen-ka.
ちょっと　寄っていきませんか。
(Why don't you drop in on us for a while?)
Chikaku-ni oide-no setsu-wa doozo oyori-kudasai.
(Please drop by when you happen to be in the neighborhood [written on a postcard announcing a change of address].)

Yoru is also used with adjectives and verbs:

chikai (near) — *chika-yoru* (approach)
motsu (bring) — *mochi-yoru* (bring things together [for a party, etc.])
kakaru (depend) — *yori-kakaru* (lean against)

. . . *ni kansuru* (concerning . . .)

Mr. Lerner was explaining a proposal of his to several senior people in the company. He thought he should use formal expressions in such a situation, so he said,

Kore-wa hiyoo-ni kanshite watashi-no iken-desu.

meaning "this is my opinion concerning the cost." Later Mr. Takada said *kanshite* should have been replaced by *kansuru*.

* * *

Several phrases including the *te* form of a verb are used to indicate a relationship between things:

. . . *ni kanshite* (concerning . . .)
. . . *ni yotte* (depending on . . .)
. . . *ni oite* (at/in . . .)
. . . *ni totte* (to/for . . .)
. . . *ni taishite* (to/against . . .)

These phrases are mainly used in formal speech or written language.

When such phrases are used with a verb, the . . .*te* form is used:

Rainen-no keekaku-ni tsuite setsumee-itashimasu.
(I will explain now about next year's plans.)
Hiyoo-ni kanshite toogi-o kasanemashita.
(We had repeated discussions concerning the cost.)

But when these phrases are used to modify a noun, different forms are used:

```
. . . ni kanshite   —   . . . ni kanshite-no/kansuru
. . . ni taishite   —   . . . ni taishite-no/taisuru
. . . ni totte      —   . . . ni totte-no
. . . ni yotte      —   . . . ni yoru
. . . ni oite       —   . . . ni oite-no/okeru
```

In the case of . . . *ni kanshite* and . . . *ni taishite*, either . . . *ni* . . . *te-no* or ". . . *ni* plus dictionary form" is used:

Kare-ni taishite-no/taisuru hinan-wa dandan tsuyoku
彼に　対しての／対する　非難

natta.
(Opposition against him steadily intensified.)

Thus Mr. Lerner should have said *Kore-wa hi-yoo-ni kansuru/kanshite-no watashi-no iken-desu.*

This distinction between adverbial form and noun-modifying form is seen in other daily phrases as well:

Eki-no mae-ni kissaten-ga arimasu.
駅の　前に　喫茶店が　あります。
(There is a coffee shop in front of the station.)
Eki-no mae-no kissaten-ni haitta.
駅の　前の　喫茶店に　入った。
(I entered the coffee shop that is in front of the station.)

Expressions meaning 'to me, for me'

Mr. Lerner received a package from his mother last week; she sent him some cookies she had made. He took some of them to the office and gave them to Miss Yoshida, saying,

Haha-ga watashi-ni okurimashita.

meaning "My mother sent them to me." She thanked him lavishly, but a few hours later she told him that

Haha-ga okutte-kimashita.
母ガ　送ってきました。

would have sounded much better.

*　　*　　*

Sentences like

Haha-ga watashi-ni okurimashita.
or
Tanaka-san-ga watashi-ni denwa-shimashita.
(**Mr. Tanaka called me.**)

can be understood but sound like they are translated directly from English.

In natural Japanese *watashi-ni* is used only when the phrase needs some emphasis. One might say something like

Imooto-ni okutta-n-ja nakute, watashi-ni okutta-n-de-su.

(She didn't send it to my sister; she sent it to **ME**.)

150

One does not say *watashi-ni* when simply stating that someone has sent him something. One usually uses either . . . *te-kureru/kudasaru* or . . . *te-kuru* instead of *watashi-ni* . . .

Haha-ga okutte-kuremashita.

is used when the speaker is particularly grateful for his mother's action.

Haha-ga okutte-kimashita.

is used when simply stating that his mother sent it to him.

. . . *te-kuru* means that the action is done by someone toward the speaker:

Yuube Tanaka-san-ga denwa-shite-kita.
田中さんが　電話してきた
(Mr. Tanaka called me last night.)
Tegami-de monku-o itte-kita.
(He wrote to me complaining about it.)

Sometimes the agent is left out when it is obvious:

Uchi-kara ringo-o okutte-kimashita.
うちから　りんごを　送ってきました。
(My family sent me apples.)
Kaisha-kara shirasete-kimashita.
(The company informed me about it.)

151

Gaman-suru (to be patient, to endure)

Mr. Lerner was having dinner at the Takadas last Saturday. When serving coffee after the meal, Mrs. Takada told her husband that she had accidentally dropped his cup that afternoon. She apologized and said,

Kore-de gaman-shite-kudasai-ne.

while showing him the coffee cup. Mr. Lerner realized that *gaman-suru* can be used to mean "to be satisfied with something not the best."

*   *   *

The verb *gaman-suru* means "to endure, to be patient." An average Japanese will associate this word with some memory from his childhood, when his mother often said *gaman-shinasai* (be patient) to him. When a child wants a sweet before a meal, his mother will say

Moo sugu gohan-da-kara gaman-shinasai.
(Be patient and wait until our meal.)

Or, when a child urges his mother to buy him a new toy, she will say

Imano-de gaman-shinasai.
今ので　がまんしなさい。
(Be satisfied with the ones you have now.)

This usage is the same as that Mrs. Takada used in referring to her husband's coffee cup.

Gaman-suru reflects the stoic idea that one should try to forbear a certain amount of pain, shortage or inconvenience. Most Japanese who are middle-aged or older have experienced material shortage and been told to be patient; they often complain that young people nowadays do not know how to *gaman-suru* because they have been brought up in an overly affluent society.

Gaman-suru can also mean "to suppress oneself psychologically":

Kattena koto-o yuu-kedo, byoonin-da-kara gaman-
病人だから　がまん
shite-yaroo.
してやろう
(I'll try to be patient with her selfish demands, since she is sick now.)

Kimi-wa gaman-ga tarinai-kara sugu kenka-suru.
がまんが　足りない
(You easily start quarreling. You need more self-restraint.)

Gaman-zuyoi がまんづよい (*lit.* strong in perseverance) is used to praise untiring efforts:

Saigo-niwa gaman-zuyoi mono-ga katsu.
(The one who perseveres will win in the end.)
Kono kooshoo-wa muzukashii-kara gaman-zuyoku yaranakya.
(These negotiations are very tough. We must be patient and tenacious.)

Kochira (this side, me)

Mr. Lerner wanted to take Mr. Okada to a restaurant he knew and asked him if he was free the next Friday. Mr. Okada looked at his schedule and said,

Kochira-wa kekkoo-desu.
こちらは　けっこうです。

He understood that the date was all right with Mr. Okada, but he wondered if he could have said *Watashi-wa kekkoo-desu* as well.

    *   *   *

Kochira, which literally means "this direction" is often used to mean "I, me" or "we, us." Mr. Okada could have said *watashi-wa* instead of *kochira-wa*, but he probably chose *kochira-wa* because he wanted to emphasize "my side" in contrast with "your side."

When meeting someone for the first time, one usually greets him with *Doozo yoroshiku* ("How do you do?" — *lit.* "Please be good to me"), and the other person will either repeat the same expression or say

Kochira-koso (doozo yoroshiku).
こちらこそ　（どうぞ　よろしく）。

to mean "It's ME that should say so."

Or, when one has apologized for something that is one's fault, the other person will often say

Kochira-koso (shitsuree-shimashita).

meaning "I should be the one to apologize."

154

Just as *kochira* is used to mean "my side," *sochira* is used to mean "your side" and *achira* "his/her side." These words are often used in place of pronouns like *watashi*, *anata* and *ano-hito*.

Sochira-no ii-yoo-ni kimete-kudasatte kamaimasen.
(You can go ahead and decide as you like.)
Achira-ga warui-n-da-kara, kochira-ga ayamaru hitsuyoo-wa nai.
あちらが わるいんだから、こちらが あやまる 必要は ない。
(Since he is in the wrong, there is no need for me to apologize.)

In familiar speech, *kotchi, sotchi, atchi* are used in place of *kochira, sochira, achira*.

Kotchi-wa ii-kedo, sotchi-wa doo?
こっちは いいけど、そっちは どう？
(I don't mind. What about you?)

Use of these words is one of the reasons that pronouns like *watashi*, *anata*, *ano-hito*, *kare* are not used where a foreigner is apt to expect them.

GENERAL INDEX

Volumes 6-10

I.   **SITUATIONAL EXPRESSIONS** .. 158
     Advice
     Apology
     Daily greetings
     Gratitude
     How to talk
     Inquiry
     Request
     Responses

II.   **WORDS & EXPRESSIONS** 160
     Adjectives and adjectival expressions
     Adverbs and adverbial expressions
     Expressions
     Idiomatic expressions
     Interjections
     Onomatopoeic words and mimicry words
     Particles and particle-like phrases
     Personal terms
     Sentence endings
     Sentence structure
     Socially significant terms
     Suffix, counters, prefix
     Verbs and verbal expressions

III. **CUSTOMS & HABITS** 165

IV. **MISCELLANEOUS** 166
     Pronunciation
     Miscellaneous

I. SITUATIONAL EXPRESSIONS

Advice

advice, expressions of
    VIII 54-5, 64-5
. . . tara doo-desu-ka   VIII 55
. . . tara ikaga-desu-ka   VIII 55

Apology

apologies for calling   VIII 94-5
apologizing for being late VIII 72-3
apology about previous
    meeting   VI 12-3
apology and kara   X 112-3
apology, expressions of
    VIII 50-1/IX 31/X 112-3
Doomo sumimasen.   IX 109
Gomen-nasai.   IX 81
Mooshiwake arimasen.   VII 17, 72-3
Ocha-mo sashiagemasen-de.   VI 25
Ojikan-o torimashita.   VI 19
Sumimasen.   VII 14, 72-3/IX 109
Warui-(wa)ne.   VI 38
Warukatta-(wa)ne.   VI 39

Daily greetings

Arigatoo-gozaimashita.   VI 38
Arigatoo-gozaimasu.   IX 108
Doomo arigatoo.   IX 108
Doomo sumimasen.   IX 109
Doozo goyukkuri.   VIII 114
Doozo sono mama.   VIII 19
Doozo yoroshiku.   VI 8/IX 68
Gokigen yoo.   VI 29
Gokuroosama.   VI 63
Gomen-kudasai (mase).   VI 15, 19
Gomen-nasai.   IX 81
Honno kimochi-desu.   VI 50-1
Itte-mairimasu.   VI 16-7
Itte-rasshai.   VI 16-7
Ja, mata.   VI 14, 63
Kochira . . . desu.   VI 8
Kochira-koso.   VI 8
Kochira-koso totsuzen
    ojama-shimashite.   VI 25
Maido arigatoo-gozaimasu.   VI 62
Makoto-ni tsumaranai
    mono-desu-ga.   VI 30
Mooshiwake arimasen.
    VII 17, 72-3/IX 109
Mooshiwake nai-n-desu-ga.
    VIII-103/IX 22

Moo takusan-desu.   VIII 118-9
. . . niwa osewa-ni natte-orimasu. VI 10
Ocha-mo sashiagemasen-de.   VI 25
Ojikan-o torimashite.   VI 19
Okaeri-nasai.   VI 120
Okagesama-de.   VI 39
Onegai-(ita)shimasu.
    VI 23, 38/VIII 107/IX 108
Osoreirimasu.   VI 38
Osoreirimasu-ga/kedo.   VIII 107
Otsukaresama.   VI 63
Oyasumi-nasai.   VI 120/IX 81
Sayonara.   VI 14-5, 16, 19
Senjitsu-wa gochisoosama-
    deshita.   VI 12
Shitsuree-desu-ga.   VIII 150-1
Shitsuree-shimasu.   VI 15, 19
Soo-deshoo-ka.   VII 132-3/VIII 9
Sumimasen.   VII 14, 72-3/IX 109
Sumimasen-deshita.   VI 39
Taihen-desu-ne.   VII 48-9
Warui-n-da/desu-kedo.   IX 22
Warui-(wa)ne.   VI 38
Warukatta-(wa)ne.   VI 39
Yoroshiku.   VI 30
Yoroshiku doozo.   IX 68-9

Gratitude

Arigatoo-gozaimashita.   VI 38
Arigatoo-gozaimasu.   IX 108
Doomo arigatoo.   IX 108
Gokuroosama.   VI 63
gratitude about previous
    meetings   VI 12-3
gratitude for help   VI 38-9
Maido arigatoo-gozaimasu.   VI 62
. . . niwa osewa-ni natte-
    orimasu   VI 10
Osoreirimasu.   VI 38
repeated expression of
    gratitude   VI 13
Senjitsu-wa gochisoosama-
    deshita.   VI 12
Tasukarimashita.   VI 132
thanking someone for his
    kindness to one's family
    member   VI 11

How to talk

aizuchi
    VI-61/VII-19, 96-7, 142-3/VIII 98-9

aizuchi-bijin	VII 142-3
aizuchi giver	VII 143
adopting children's terms	VII 125
answering with phrases	VII 118-9
anticipating what follows	X 114-5
completing someone's un-finished statement	VI 81
conversation opening	VI 10-1, 42
conveying a message	VII 58-9
conveying someone's order	VII 93
checking someone's comprehension	IX 54-5
confirming someone's statement	IX 56-7, 98-9
correcting others	IX 22-3
dangling tone	VI 69
denial, strong	VI 36-7
different attitude in the speaker's part	VI 76-7
emphasizing the negation	VIII 146-7
emphasizing the speaker's intentions or judgment	VIII 16-7
end of business discussions	VI 18-9
ending telephone conversations	VIII 102-3
formal speech	X 8-9
humble speech	VIII 148-9
indirect development of conversation	VII 100-1
indirect request	VII 100-1
inviting conversation	VIII 100-1
last part of a sentence can be understood	X 135
listener anticipating what will come next	VI 133
listener participating in completing the speaker's sentences	VI 137
looking for the right expression	VIII 110-1
making a question sound less demanding	VIII 8-9
male speech used toward women	VII 124-5
opening a conversation	VII 118-9
physical distance between the speakers	VI 126-7
polite expressions of opposition	VII 132-3
polite refusal	VIII 48-9
polite requests	VII 56-7
polite questions	VIII 52-3
politely asking about someone's opinion or wishes	VIII 8-9
preliminary remarks	VII 41
repeating similar expressions	VI 19
replying to praise	VIII 106-7

responding to a compliment	VI 42-3
saying good-bye in a telephone conversation	VIII 102-3
showing the speaker's reserve in expressing his opinion	VIII 10-1
signals to show that one is going to start talking	VI 130
silence to show hesitation	VII 133
sounding hesitant or apologetic when making a request	VI 27
speaker and listener participating in a flow of speech	VI 81
speaker's attitude	VI 134-5
speaker's control	VI 72-3
starting a business discussion	VI 112-3
starting a statement	VII 126-7
suggestion, making a	VII 52-3
talking to oneself	VII 25, 144
unexpected development in conversation	VII 102-3
using a greater number of steps	VI 127

Inquiry

asking about someone's wishes	VI 58/VIII 20-1
asking how to read someone's name in kanji	VIII 143
asking someone's name	VIII 150
ikimasu-ka vs. *ikimasen-ka*	VI 22-3

Request

asking for advice	VIII 58-9
asking for explanation	IX 52-3
asking for instructions	VI 58-9/VIII 142-3/IX 20-1
asking someone to return a phone call	VI 32-3
indirect requests	VII 100-1
making a request in a reserved way	VI 26-7
making requests	VIII 24-5, 150-1/IX 14-5, 26-7
. . . *naide-(kudasai/ne)*	IX 142, 154
Onegai-(ita)shimasu.	VI 23,38
sounding hesitant or apologetic when making a request	VI 27
. . . *te-hoshii*	VIII 108-9
. . . *te-itadakenai-deshoo-ka*	IX 119
. . . *te-kudasai*	IX 14-5, 26, 46, 154
. . . *te-moraenai-kana*	IX 118-9
. . . *te-ne*	IX 46-7, 100-1
. . . *te-yo*	IX 46-7
Yoroshiku onegai-shimasu.	IX 108

159

Responses

aizuchi
VI 61/VII 19, 96-7, 142-3/VIII 98-9
Hai and Soo-desu VII 88-9
hai implying you want to termi-
nate the conversation VII 96-7
hai used to call someone's
attention to an action VII 97

hai used to show polite
attitude VII 88-9
hai, various uses of VII 96-7
polite refusal VIII 48-9, 152-3
replying to praise VIII 106-7
responding to compliments
VII 30-1
responding to invitation-like
comments VIII 160-1

II. WORDS & EXPRESSIONS

**Adjectives and adjectival
expressions**

aa-yuu VII 8
anna VI 150-1/VII 8-9
ano VI 150-1
atsui (hon) IX 136-7
benri IX 132
chiisai IX 126
"convenient," expressions
meaning IX 132-3
donna VII 8-9
donna vs. doo-yuu VII 9
expressions ending in . . . nna
VII 8-9
fuben IX 132
futoi IX 136
fuyukai IX 62
gaman-zuyoi X 153
genki VIII 82-3
go + adjectives VIII 43
honno VI 50-1
hosoi IX 137
joozu IX 72-3
juubun IX 112-3
kekkoo VIII 152, 155/X106-7
kenkoo VIII 83
kinben VIII 83
kono VI 150-1
koo-yuu VII 8-9
kurushii and tsurai X 130-1
o + adjectives VIII 42-3
omoshiroku nai IX 62
onajimi VIII 46-7
ookii and ookina X 56-7
semai IX 126-7
"small," expressions
meaning IX 126-7
sonna VI 117/VIII 79
sono VI 150-1
sono vs. ano VI 150-1
subarashii IX 73
taihen IX 77
taihen, uses of VIII 68-9

taishita VI 37
tanoshii VIII 114-5
te form of adjectives IX 130-1
umai IX 72-3
ureshii VI 90-1
ureshii and koofuku X 40-1
usui IX 136-7

**Adverbs and adverbial
expressions**

amari X 76-7
chan-to VII 88-9
chotto VI 22/VII 11, 133/VIII 79
dooka VIII 101
doozo VIII 100-1/VII 17
honto-ni VIII 36,60
kitto VIII 48
mada VIII 140
maido VIII 46-7
makoto-ni VIII 22
mattaku VIII 36
mochiron VI 144-5
moo, uses of VIII 140-1
nakanaka VIII 82
nandaka VIII 10-1, 126
nandemo VIII 12-3
sappari VIII 120-1
satto VI 140-1
sorosoro VIII 34
tabun VI 94-5
takusan, uses of VIII 118-9
zehi VIII 14-5, 60-1
zuibun VIII 118

Expressions

accompanying an action VII 130-1
describing being hurt
in a fall VI 146-7
describing change VII 54-5
describing disappointment
or irritation VII 39
describing headache VI 46-7

describing stomachache VI 44-5
implying "too much" VIII 130-1
indicating certainty about
  what will happen in the
  future VIII 14
indicating gratitude
  VII 70-1/VIII 84
indicating gratitude for
  someone's help VII 38-9/X 14-5
indicating one's desires VIII 14
indicating one's will and
  wishes VIII 14-5
indicating the cause of
  emotion X 128-9
indicating the speaker's
  emotions vividly VIII 30-1
indicating the subject VI 152-3
meaning "almost" X 20-1
meaning "as you know" VI 40-1
meaning "but" X 46-7
meaning "convenient" IX 132-3
meaning "Don't . . ." IX 154-5
meaning "enjoy" VIII 114-5
meaning "everything" X 36-7
meaning "finish . . . ing" VIII 134-5
meaning "Have a good . . ."
  VIII 114-5
meaning "I think that . . ." X 116-7
meaning "I would like
  you to . . ." VIII 108-9
meaning "Isn't it?" X 38-9
meaning "just as it is now"
  VIII 19-20
meaning "not at all" VI 30, 114-5
meaning "why" X 28-9
of ability and inability to
  do something IX 82-3
of advice VIII 54-5, 64-5
of anger IV 62-3
of apology VIII 50-1/IX 31/X 112-3
of apology or gratitude about
  previous meeting VI 12-3
of approximate numer VIII 90-1
of confirmation VIII 66-7
of consent VIII 26-7
of existence VIII 136-7
of gratitude VIII 84
of gratitude and compliments
  VI 11
of "must" VII 126-7
of losing things IX 88-9
of pain X 130-1
of "please accept it" VI 30
of pleasure VI 90-1
of regret IX 31, 44-5
of sarcasm VII 141
of "should have" X 80-1
of sympathy VIII 69
of "to me, for me" X 150-1
used at the end of business

discussions VI 18-9
used for idling away
  one's time VIII 62-3
used for accepting an offer VII 16-7
used for admiration X 18-9
used for praise X 94-5
used for reporting VII 58-9
used for starting
  a statement VI 126-7
used for strong denial VI 116-7
used when offering a gift VIII 22-3

Idiomatic expressions

ai-ni iku/kuru IX 124-5
asobi-ni iku/kuru IX 124-5
atama-ni kuru IX 62
. . . (ta) bakari VI 47/VII 146-7
. . . eba ii-deshoo VIII 142-3
hara-ga tatsu IX 62
. . . hazu-ga nai VI 116/VIII 78
hyotto suru-to VI 94
ichigai-niwa ienai IX 59
ii kagen VIII 84-5
ii tokoro VI 100-1
. . . (ta) ijoo (now that)
  VIII 80-1/IX 8-9
ima hitotsu X 110-1
ima ichi X 111
imadoki VIII 88-9
imasara VIII 78-9
. . . kko nai VI 116-7
kokoro-bakari-no VIII 48
korekara . . . tokoro VII 78
koto used to mean "necessity"
  VI 98-9
koto-ni yoru-to VI 94
. . . (ta) mama IX 37
ma-ni au IX 113
mi-ni iku IX 125
mon(o)-desu-ka VI 116
moo . . . kirenai VIII 131
moo sukoshi-de . . . (suru)
  tokoro-datta VI 101
moshika shitara VI 94-5
moshika suru-to VI 94-5
nandemo . . . soo-desu VIII 12-3
nani-kara nani-made VIII 33
. . . nanka VI 153
nantoka X 12-3
nantoka . . . dekiru VI 126-7
. . . nashi-de IX 142-3
. . . ni chigainai IX 104
. . . no koto VII 154-5
. . . no mama IX 37
. . . nomo shikata-ga nai VII 139
oisogashii tokoro VII 79
onegai-da-kara VII 46-7
otesuu-desu-ga VII 17
sekkaku . . . noni VI 77

sekkaku-desu-kara	VIII 150-1
shoochi-shimashita	VIII 27
. . . soo-mo nai	IX 85
soo-yuu koto-de	VI 18
. . . suru koto-ga aru	VI 98-9
. . . suru koto-ni naru	VI 98-9
. . . suru koto-ni suru	VI 98-9
. . . ta hoo-ga ii	VII 24-5/VIII 54-5,65
tanomu-kara	VII 46-7
. . . tara doo-desu-ka	VIII 58
. . . tara ikaga-desu-ka	VIII 58
. . . (suru)-to ii	VIII 54-5
. . . to iimashite-mo	VII 77
. . . to kitara	IX 110-1
. . . to omoimashite/omotte	VII 56-7
. . . to yuu hanashi-desu	VII 43
. . . to yuu koto-desu	VII 43,59
. . . to yuu koto-ni narimasu-ne	IX 57
. . . to yuu wake-desu	VII 122
tokoro	IX 122-3
. . . (ta) tokoro	VII 79, 146-7
toshi-desu	VIII 124-5
toshi-ni niawazu	VIII 125
tsui . . . te-shimau	VIII 128-9
. . . ttara ani	IX 87
. . . yori shikata-ga nai	VII 138

Interjections

ano-ne	VI 10-1, 26
anoo	VI 10-1, 26
anoo vs. eeto	VII 110-1
bai-bai	VI 15
banzai	VIII 96-7
moshimoshi	VIII 98-9
oi	VII 11

Onomatopoeic words and mimicry words

batan	VI 141
boketto	VIII 63
bootto	VIII 63
burabura(-suru)	VI 93/VIII 62-3
doshidoshi	VI 46
doshindoshin	VI 46
gangan	VI 47
gorogoro	VII 65/VIII 62-3
gorori, gorotto	VII 65
hirihiri	VII 49
kirikiri	VI 44,46
nikoniko, nikotto	VII 65
pikapika	VII 64-5
pikari(-to)	VII 64-5
pikatto	VII 64-5
pittari	VI 140-1
shikushiku	VI 44

sorosoro	VIII 34
zaazaa	VI 141
zukinzukin	VI 46
zukizuki	VI 46, 49

Particles and particle-like phrases

. . . dake	IX 28-9
. . . dano . . . dano	X 132-3
. . . de	IX 106-7, 121
. . . de (ii)	IX 112-3
. . . de (juubun)	IX 112-3
. . . de vs. . . . ni	VIII 116-7
. . . e	IX 121
. . . e vs. . . . ni	VIII 116-7
iku-yo vs. iku-wayo	VII 95
. . . koso	VII 150-1
leaving out particles	IX 107, 120-1
. . . made	IX 121
. . . ne	VII 26-7
. . . ni	IX 120-1, 124-5
. . . ni vs. . . . tame-ni	IX 114-5
. . . ni kansuru/kanshite	X 148-9
. . . ni . . . ni	X 44-5
. . . ni oite/okeru	X 148-9
. . . ni taisuru/taishite	X 148-9
. . . ni totte	X 64-5
. . . ni yoru	IX 58-9
. . . no koto vs. . . . ni tsuite	VIII 132-3
. . . none	IX 56-7
. . . noni vs. . . . keredomo	VI 96-7
. . . o	IX 106-7, 120-1
particles at the end of sentences	VIII 30-1
particles meaning "in/at," etc.	VIII 116-7
particles meaning "to"	VIII 138-9
sentence particle, pronunciation of	VIII 92-3
. . . shika	IX 29
sore-de vs. sore-dewa	VI 136-7
. . . ta ato-de vs. . . . te-kara	X 88-9
. . . to	X 132-3
. . . to vs. . . . toka	VIII 76-7
. . . toka	VIII 116-7/X 50-1
. . . wa	VII 44-5
. . . wa and . . . mo	X 114-5
. . . wa, leaving out	VI 153
. . . wa, used at the end of a sentence	VIII 16-7
. . . wa used to mean "not at all"	VI 114-5
. . . wa vs. . . . ga	VI 78-9
. . . wane	VIII 17, 67
. . . wayo	VIII 17
watashi-wa vs. watashi-ga	VI 78-9
. . . ya	X 132-3
. . . ya vs. . . . toka	VIII 77
. . . yori	IX 121

Personal terms

addressing someone by name
    X 16-7, 58-9
anata   VII 128-9
hito   VII 149
kanai vs. *tsuma*   VI 28
okusan   VII 129
onna vs. *onna-no-hito*   VI 132
otoko vs. *otoko-no-hito*   VI 132
tsuma   VI 28
tsure   VI 22

Sentence endings

. . . *ka(na)*   VII 144-5
. . . *kashira*   VII 13,73
. . . *na* (used as familiar
    confirmation)   VIII 66-7
. . . *na* (used when talking
    to oneself)   VIII 30-1, 66
. . . *n-desu-kedo*   VII 13
. . . *ne*   VII 26-7
. . . *ne*, added to particles   VII 153
. . . *ne*, phrases with   VII 152-3
. . . *ne* vs. . . . *wane*   VII 95
. . . *nee*   VII 10-1
. . . *n-ja nai-deshoo-ka*   VII 132
particles at the end of
    sentences   VIII 30-1
reserved endings   VII 132-3
sentence endings in familiar
    conversation   VII 94-5

Sentence structure

adverbs anticipating a
    negative statement   VIII 78-9
anata, unnecessary   VII 128-9
answering with phrases   VII 118-9
avoiding long modifiers   VII 18-9
common contractions   VII 34-5
connecting two sentences
    VII 36-7, 62-3
concecutive actions   IX 12-3
continued topic   VII 100-1
dictionary form + *na*   IX 154-5
double negative   VIII 146-7
emphasizing adjectives &
    verbs   VIII 126-7
emphasizing completion of
    an action   IX 44-5
expressions indicating
    the subject   VI 152-3
first part of a sentence
    implying the rest   VI 132-3
. . . *ga nai* vs. . . . *ja nai*   VIII 82-3
go + noun/stem of verb   IX 26-7
hidden sentence subjects   VII 100-5

ikemasen left out   VII 98-9
imperative in indirect
    speech   VII 92-3
indicating subject matter
    IX 110-1, 116-7
introductory words with
    . . . *ka*   VII 20-1
last part of a sentence can
    be understood   X 134-5
leaving out a verb phrase   VII 48-9
leaving out particles   IX 107, 120-1
length of sentences   VII 18-9
leaving out the last part
    VII 56-7, 66-7
making verbs from adjectives
    X 24-5
narimasen left out   VII 98-9
. . . *n-desu-ka*   IX 64-5
ne used between phrases   VII 112-3
negative form in questions
    VII 22-3, 114-5
negative imperative   VII 154-5
. . . *no mae-ni* vs. . . . *no mae-no*
    X 149
noun + *desu*   VII 136-7
o . . . ni naru   IX 66-7
. . . *o* often dropping   VII 87
o + stem + *desu-ka*   VII 134-5
passive form   VI 54
phrases ending with . . . *te*   VII 12-3
plain imperative   VI 82/VII 92-3
position of phrases indicating
    numbers   VI 129
potential form   IX 82, 102-3
rhetorical questions   VII 116-7
sentence subject   VII 152-3
something that the speaker
    cannot control   VI 72-3
subjects determined only by
    the situation   VII 105
subjects indicated by the
    use of humble expression VII 103
subjects indicated by the
    of polite terms   VII 102-3
subjects obvious from the
    situation   VII 104-5
suffering from someone's
    actions   VI 54-5
ta form   VI 38-9
. . . *ta* used to indicate the
    completion of an action VI 74-5
te form of adjectives   IX 130-1
te form used with expres-
    sions of apology and
    gratitude   VIII 50-1
. . . *wa*, leaving out   VI 153
wa used to indicate
    contrast   VII 106-7
watashi-ga vs. *watashi-wa* VI 78-9
"you" in Japanese   VII 128-9

163

Socially significant terms

achira	X 155
ariawase	VI 51
. . . kankee	X 30-1
kochira	X 154-5
meeshi	VI 9
sochira	X 155
tema	X 126-7
tesuu	X 127
yatsu	X 10-1

Suffix, counters, prefix

. . . ageru	VIII 134-5
. . . atsukai	X 26-7
. . . chotto	X 20
. . . chuu and . . . juu	X 54-5
counter for people	VIII 28-9
counters, use of	VIII 74-5
. . . darake	X 70-1
. . . dasu vs. . . . . hajimeru	VI 112-3
. . . do meaning "times"	VII 52
. . . dooshi	X 100-1
. . . gachi	X 62-3
. . . hiki (counter)	VIII 74-5
. . . hodo	X 8-9
. . . hon (counter)	VIII 74
ichido vs. ikkai	X 144-5
. . . kankee	X 30-1
. . . kirenai	VI 115
. . . kiru	VIII 134-5
. . . komu	VI 122
. . . mai (counter)	VIII 75
. . . mase	VI 30
. . . mee(-sama)	VIII 28-9
. . . mono	X 74-5
. . . nikui	VII 84-5
. . . nin (counter)	VIII 75
. . . owaru	VIII 134-5
. . . ppanashi	IX 36-7
. . . ppoi	VI 110-1
. . . sama	VIII 28-9
suu- (several)	VIII 90-1
. . . tai (counter)	VIII 75
. . . te (person)	X 142-3
. . . too (counter)	VIII 74
. . . tsuu (counter)	VIII 75
. . . wa (counter)	VIII 74
. . . ya (familiar sentence particle)	X 92-3
. . . ya (person)	X 66-7
. . . yori (close to)	X 146-7

Verbs and verbal expressions

ageru	VIII 34-5
-areru (respect)	VI 12-3
aru used for human beings	VIII 136-7

causative form	VIII 40-1
. . . cha	VII 34-5
. . . cha ikenai/dame	IX 155
. . . chatta	VII 34-5
chuushi-suru vs. chuushi-ni naru	X 60-1
. . . de irassharu	VII 23/VIII 44-5
dekakeru	IX 114
. . . deshita-ka vs. . . . . desu-ka	VIII 8-9
. . . deshitara	IX 116-7
. . . deshoo	IX 51
. . . desu-ga/kedo	IX 31
. . . eba vs. . . . tara, . . . to	IX 60-1
gaman-suru	X 152-3
haitte-iru vs. irete-aru	VI 134-5
hanashikakeru	VI 118-9
hanashikomu	VI 123
higamu	VI 111
ikimashita vs. kimashita	VII 117
ikimasu vs. ikimashoo	VII 74
ikimasu-ka vs. ikimasen-ka	VII 22-3
ikiru	VII 50-1
iku	IX 114-5
iku toki vs. itta toki	VI 75
imperative form	IX 80-1, 154
iru	VIII 116-7
kaeru toki vs. kaetta toki	VI 74-5
kagi-ga kakatte-iru	X 72-3
kagiru vs. kagiranai	IX 34-5
komaru	IX 104
komaru/komarimasu used in a reprimand	VII 90-1
komatte-iru/imasu	VII 91
korobu	VI 150-1
. . . koto-ga dekinai	IX 82-3, 84
kotowaru	X 104-5
. . . ku naru vs. . . . ni naru	X 150-1
kudasai	IX 26-7
kudasaru	VI 53
kureru	VI 53
kuru	IX 114-5
. . . masen-deshita	VI 70-1
mitsukaru vs. mitsukeru	VII 60-1
nakusu	IX 88
naosu vs. naoru	IX 70-1
narimasen	VII 126-7
narimasen left out	VII 98-9
naru	VII 54-5
. . . negaimasu	IX 26-7
. . . ni suginai	X 106-7
nomimasen vs. nomemasen	IX 75
nonbiri-suru	VI 93
o + stem form of verbs	VIII 144-5, 148-9
okoru	IX 62-3
omoidasanai vs. omoidasenai	IX 74-5
osawagase-suru	VIII 46-7
oshiete-itadaku	VIII 58-9
otosu	IX 88

164

potential form	IX 82, 102-3	. . . te-mitara	IX 12-3
sareru	VI 66-7	. . . te-moraenai-kana	IX 118-9
. . . saseru vs. . . . te-morau	VIII 40-1	. . . te-ne	VI 80-1, 85
sumu	VIII 116-7	. . . te-oku	VI 135
surimuku	VI 49	. . . te-shimau	IX 44-5
suru used to mean "to cost"	VI 92-3	. . . te-wa used to indicate	
susumeru	IX 97	condition	VI 86-7
. . . ta used to completion		. . . te-wa vs. . . . eba	VI 86-7
of an action	VI 74-5	. . . te-wa ikemasen	VI 83, 87
tabena vs. taberu-na	VI 84	. . . te-wa komarimasu	VI 87
tanoshimu	VIII 114-5	"to become," expressions	
tanomu	VII 17/VIII 116-7	meaning	IX 102-3
taoreru	VI 52-3	. . . to iimasu/mooshimasu	IX 18-9
. . . tara	VI 153/IX 12-3/X 138-9	. . . to kitara	IX 110-1
tazunete-iku/kuru	IX 125	"to visit," expressions	
tazunete-kuru	VI 52-3	meaning	IX 124-5
. . . te used to end a sentence		torareru	X 90-1
	VI 80-1	transitive and intransitive	
. . . te used to indicate a reason		verbs	IX 70-1
	VI 72-3	tsukareru	IX 104-5
. . . te vs. . . . node/kara	VI 73	tsutomeru	VIII 116-7
. . . te-ageru	IX 71	tsuujiru	IX 113
te form, pronouncing	IX 90-1	ukagau	VIII 60-1, 149, 152
. . . te-iku	VII 55	ukkari-suru	VIII 129
. . . te-imasen	VI 70-1	yareru	IX 113
. . . te-iru vs. . . . te-aru	VI 134-5	yarikirenai	IX 104-5
. . . te-itadakenai-deshoo-ka	IX 119	yaru vs. ageru	VIII 34-5
. . . te-itadaku	VI 104-5/VII 70-1	yaru vs. suru	VIII 38-9
. . . te-kudasai	IX 14-5, 26, 46, 154	. . . yoo-ni naru vs. . . . ni naru	
. . . te-kudasaru	VII 38, 71		IX 102-3
. . . te-kuru	VI 52-3/VII 55/X 98-9	. . . yoo-ni yuu	IX 96-7
. . . te-kureru	VI 53/VII 71	yoru	X 146-7
. . . te-miru	VII 80-1/IX 94-5	zonjiru	IX 148-9

III. CUSTOMS & HABITS

accepting a compliment	VII 40	calling just before one's visit	
accepting an invitation	VII 74-5		VI 64-5
accepting an offer	VIII 152-3	celebrating a victory	VIII 96-7
accepting an offer of help		chef's recommendation	VI 23
	VIII 100-1	complaints about the heat	VII 108-9
addressing a person	IX 48-9	complaints about the weather	
addressing someone	VI 23		VII 108-9
adopting children's terms	VII 125	compliments	VI 11
approving the good points that		compliment on a foreigner's	
the other person has made		Japanese	VI 42
	VIII 36-7	conveying a message	VI 34-5, 82-3
asking someone's intention/		conveying someone's order	VII 93
wishes politely	IX 50-1	declining an offer of help	VI 36-7
attributing the merit to		denial of the other person's	
someone else	VI 91	judgment or intention	VIII 104-5
avoiding generalization	IX 58-9	exchanging complaints	VII 108-9
being accepted as a foreigner		explaining the reason why	
	VII 41	one was late	VII 72-3
belittling one's gift	VI 30-1	expressing one's will	
bowing	VI 8-9, 80, 131	or wishes	VIII 14-5
calling a waitress' attention	VI 23	family language	VI 97

165

giving direction VI 56-7
giving one's card to someone VIII 112-3
giving one's name IX 18-9
giving someone's name without any terms of respect VI 29
humble speech VIII 148-9
identifying oneself with one's family members VIII 35
indicating a reason IX 10-1, 14-5
indirect expression VI 146-7
inquiring about someone's wishes VIII 20-1
introducing a relative or colleagues VIII 72-3
making sure that the other person finds it convenient to talk on the phone VIII 155
negation of a reason VI 138-9

not introducing someone by name VIII 72-3
offering to do a favor X 32-3
oseji vs. compliment VIII 106-7
physical distance between the speakers VII 126-7
praising one's family VII 40-1
praising someone's skill IX 72-3
process of receiving a gift VI 30-1
refusal to an offer VIII 152
reporting something bad VIII 69
responding to invitation-like comments VIII 60-1
telephone conversation III 94-5, 98-9, 102-3
visiting someone without notice VI 24-5
wife reporting her husband's absence from the office VI 29

IV. MISCELLANEOUS

Pronunciation

accent VI 128
contracted forms VI 106-7
dangling tone VII 119,133
devocalizing the "i" sound IX 91
dropping of the "i" sound VII 34,82-3
dropping of the "o" sound VII 86-7
"g" sound nasalized VII 115
gozaimasen sounding like gozaasen VII 114
"i" dropped in iku/itta VII 82
"i" dropped in irassharu VII 83
"i" dropped in . . . ni naru VII 83
"i" dropped in . . . te-iru VII 82
intonation of Soo-desu-ka VI 142-3
kagi vs. kani VII 115
long vowels, pronunciation of VII 112-3
"m" sound VII 114
nasalized "g" sound VII 115
no often becoming n VII 86
number of syllables VI 154-5
obasan vs. obaasan VII 113
ojisan vs. ojiisan VII 112
oo vs. oooo VII 113
phonetic changes in rapid speech VII 82-3, 86-7, 98-9
pronunciation of certain sentence pariticles VIII 92-3
pronunciation of "ka" VIII 92-3
pronunciation of the te-form IX 90-1
"u" in masu/desu devocalized VII 116-7
vowels, length of VII 112-3
voiceless vowels VII 116-7

Miscellaneous

changes in the meaning of words VI 64-5
classroom Japanese VI 58-9
common sayings VI 154-5
haiku VI 154
kakegoe VII 130
kanji compounds VI 67
paper-recycling truck announcement VIII 46-7
pronunciation making the meaning clear VI 107
pun VI 155
pun between kaeru & kaeru VII 145
quotation VII 93
redundancy VI 60-1
signs and written instruction VI 83
sharply inhaling or sucking teeth during speech VI 131
tanka VI 154
thinking in kanji VI 65
tone and the speaker's intention VI 69

INDEX TO WORDS, PHRASES AND SENTENCES

Volumes 6-10

A

aa	X 140-1
Aa, soo-desu-ka.	VIII 93
aa-yuu	VII 8
accent	VI 128
accepting a compliment	VII 40
accepting an invitation	VII 74-5
accepting an offer of help	VIII 100-1
achira	X 155
addressing a person	IX 48-9
addressing someone by name	X 16-7, 58-9
adobaisu	IX 96-7
adopting children's terms	VII 125
adverbs anticipating a negative statement	VIII 78-9
advice, expressions of	VIII 54-5, 64-5
ageru	VIII 34-5
-ageru (suffix)	VIII 134-5
ai-ni iku/kuru	IX 124-5
aitsu	X 11
aizuchi	VI 81/VII 19, 96-7, 142-3/VIII 98-9
aizuchi-bijin	VII 142-3
aizuchi-giver	VII 143
akachan vs. akanboo	VIII 34
amari . . . nai	X 76-7, 134-5
anata, unnecessary	VII 128-9
Anata-wa?	VII 128
anna	VI 150-1/VII 8-9
ano	VI 150-1
ano-ne	VII 10-1, 26
anoo	VII 10-1, 26
anoo vs. eeto	VIII 110-1
answering with phrases	VII 118-9
anticipating what follows	X 114-5
apologies for calling	VIII 94-5
apologizing for being late	VII 72-3
apology about previous meetings	VI 12-3
apology, expressions of	VIII 50-1/X 112-3
approving the good points that the other person has made	VIII 36-7
approximate number, expressions of	VIII 90-1

. . . areru (respect)	VI 66-7
ariawase	VI 51
Arigatoo-gozaimashita.	VI 38
Arigatoo-gozaimasu.	IX 108
Arigatoo.	X 14
aru (used for human beings)	VIII 116-7, 136-7
arya	VI 68
. . . asete-itadakemasen-ka	X 33
. . . asete-kudasai (masen-ka)	X 32-3
asking for explanation	IX 52-3
asking for instructions or permission	VIII 154-5
asking for instructions	VI 58-9/VIII 142-3/IX 20-1
asking for someone's opinion/advice	X 74-5
asking how to read someone's name in kanji	VIII 143
asking someone for advice	VIII 58-9
asking someone to return a phone call	VI 32-3
asking someone's intention politely	IX 66-7
asking someone's name	VIII 150
asking someone's opinion	IX 50-1
asking someone's wishes politely	VI 59/IX 66-7
asobi-ni iku/kuru	IX 124-5
atama-ni kuru	IX 62
atchi	X 155
atsui (hon)	IX 136-7
. . . atsukai	X 26-7
attributing the merit to someone else	VI 91
avoiding generalizations	IX 58-9
avoiding long modifiers	VII 18-9

B

-ba vs. -n-nara	VIII 70-1
bai-bai	VI 15
banzai	VIII 96-7
batan	VI 141
before accepting an offer	VIII 152-3
being accepted as a foreigner	VII 41
being hurt in a fall	VI 48-9
beki	VII 68-9/X 80

belittling one's gift | VI 30-1
benri | IX 132
boke-tto (shite-iru) | VIII 63
boo-tto (shite-iru) | VIII 63
bowing | VI 8-9, 80, 131
burabura (shite-iru) | VIII 62-3
burabura-suru | VI 93
byooki | VIII 82-3

C

calling a waitress' attention | VI 23
calling just before one's visit | VI 24
causative form | VIII 40-1
celebrating a victory | VIII 96-7
. . . *cha* | VII 34-5
. . . *cha ikenai/dame* | IX 155
. . . *cha iru-kedo* | VII 44
chan-to | VI 88-9
change, expressions indicating | VII 54-5
changes in the meaning of words | VI 64-5
. . . *chatta* | VII 34
checking someone's compre-
hension | IX 54-5
chef's recommendation | VI 23
chiisai | IX 126
chiisai vs. *chiisana* | X 56-7
chika-yoru | X 147
chikaku | X 20-1
(. . . *no*) *chikaku* | IX 122-3
-*choo* (counter) | IX 16
choodai-itashimasu | VIII 49
chooshi | VIII 84
Chotto . . . | VI 22
*Chotto sono hen-made mairi-
mashita-node.* | VI 24
chotto | VII 11, 133/VIII 79/IX 53/X 20-1
chuu (vs. *juu*) | X 54-5
chuukoku | IX 96-7
chuunen-no otoko | VI 132
chuushi-suru vs. *chuushi-ni naru* | X 60-1
classroom Japanese | VI 58-9
common contractions | VII 34-5
common sayings | VI 154-5
comparing two items | IX 24-5
complaints about the heat | VII 108-9
complaints about the weather | VII 108-9
completing someone's
unfinished statement | VI 81
compliments | VI 11
compliments, accepting | VII 40
compliments on a foreigner's
Japanese | VI 42

compliments, responding to | VI 42-3/VII 30-1
confirmation, expressions of | VIII 66-7
confirming someone's statement | IX 56-7
confirming what someone
has said | IX 98-9
connecting two sentences | VII 36-7, 62-3
consent, expression of | VIII 26-7
context | VI 133
continued topic | VII 100-1
contracted forms | VI 166-7
"convenient," expressions
meaning | IX 132-3
conversation opening | VI 10-1, 42
conveying a message | VII 34-5, 82-3/VII 58-9
conveying someone's order | VII 93
correcting others | IX 22-3
counter for people | VIII 28-9
counters, uses of | VIII 74-5

D

. . . -*da-to omoimasu* | VIII 11
. . . *dageru* | VII 35
daijoobu | VIII 152
dake | IX 28-9/X106
dakedo | X 46
dame-desu | VII 126-7
dane vs. *ne* | VII 94
dangling tone | VI 69/VII 119, 133
. . . *dano* . . . *dano* | X 132-3
. . . *darake* | X 70-1
dareka | VII 20-1
Dareka inai-ka-to omotte . . . | X 120
. . . *dasu* | VI 112-3
. . . *dasu* vs. . . . . *hajimeru* | VI 112-3
Dattara. . . | IX 117
. . . *dattara* | X 84-5
datte | X 47
De . . . | VII 62-3
. . . *de* | IX 106-7, 121
. . . *de (juubun)* | IX 112-3
. . . *de ippai* | X 71
. . . *de irasshaimasu-ka* vs.
. . . *de irasshaimasen-ka* | VII 23
. . . *de* vs. . . . . *ni* | VIII 116-7
De, kyoo-wa . . . | VI 20
. . . *de-irassharu* (replacing
. . . -*desu*) | VIII 44-5
. . . *de-wa* | IX 143
declining an offer of help | VI 36-7
dekakeru | IX 114
Demo . . . | X 47
. . . *demo* | VI 146-7/X 51
Demo, sore-dewa | VIII 152-3

(strong) denial of the other
  person's judgment or intention
                         VIII 104-5
(strong) denial   VI 116-7/VIII 125
denoting a reason   IX 32-3
describing being hurt in a fall
                         VI 48-9
describing headache   VI 46-7
describing stomachache VI 44-5
Deshitara . . .   X 85
. . . deshitara   IX 116-7
. . . deshoo   IX 51
. . . deshoo-ka   IX 119
. . . deshoo-ka vs. . . . . desu-ka
                         VIII 8-9
. . . desu (giving one's name) IX 19
Desu-ga . . .   X 46
. . . desu-ga/kedo. . . IX 31
. . . desu-ka (vs. . . . . n-desu-ka)
                         IX 64-5
desu-kedo   X 47
desu-mono   VI 96-7
. . . desu-ne   VII 27/IX 98-9
devocalizing the "i" sound   IX 91
Dewa, kore-de shitsuree-shimasu.
                         VI 25
Dewa, kore-de.   VI 16
different attitude in the
  speaker's part   VI 76-7
disappointment or irritation VII 39
-do meaning time(s) VII 52/X 144-5
dochira-sama   VIII 150
Dochirasama-deshoo-ka.   VIII 8-9
. . . doita   VII 35
doitsu   X 11
Dokkoisho!   VII 131
dokoka   VII 20-1
"Don't . . .," expressions
  meaning   IX 154-5
donata (-sama)   VIII 150
donna   VII 8-9
donna hito vs. doo-yuu hito VII 9
Donna mon-deshoo-ka.   X 74
doo   IX 51/X 140-1
doo . . . eba ii-deshoo   VI 58-9
Doo-deshoo-ka.   X 74
Doo-desu-ka.   X 74
doo-yuu   VI 157/VII 8-9
dooka   VIII 101
doomo (somehow)   IX 53
Doomo arigatoo.   IX 108
Doomo osawagase-shimashita.
                         VIII 46
Doomo sumimasen.   IX 109
doomo   VII 133/VIII 79, 107
. . . doori   IX 40-1
. . . dooshi   X 100-1
dooshite   X 28-9
doozo   VII 17
doozo (vs. dooka)   VIII 100-1

doozo (vs. "please")   VIII 100-1
Doozo goyukkuri.   VIII 114-5
Doozo ogenki-de.   IX 39
Doozo sono mama.   VIII 19
Doozo yoroshiku.   VI 8/IX 68
dore-mo kore-mo   VIII 33
doreka   VII 20
doshidoshi   VI 46
doshindoshin   VI 46
double negative   VIII 146-7
dropping of the "i" sound
                      VII 34, 82-3
dropping of the "o" sound VII 86-7

                 E

. . . e (vs. . . . made)   X 78-9
. . . e   IX 121
. . . e vs. . . . ni   VIII 138-9
. . . eba   X 138-9
. . . eba (vs. . . . tara, to) IX 60-1
. . . eba ii-deshoo   VIII 142-3
. . . eba yokatta (-noni) X 80-1
eeto vs. anoo   VIII 110-1
emphasizing adj. & verbs
                         VIII 126-7
emphasizing completion of
  action   IX 44-5
emphasizing the negation
                         VIII 146-7
emphasizing the speaker's
  intentions or judgment VIII 16-7
end of business discussions VI 18-9
ending telephone conversations
                         VIII 102-3
erai   X 94-5
evaluation   VI 89
exchanging complaints VII 108-9
existence, expressions of
                         VIII 136-7
expectations   VI 88-9
explaining the reason why one
  was late   VII 72-3
expressing ability and inability
  to do something   IX 82-3
expressing apology   IX 31
expressing gratitude for service
                         X 14-5
expressing inability to do
  something (with reserve)
                         IX 84-5
expressing one's anger   IX 62-3
expressing one's desires VIII 14
expressing one's will and wishes
                         VIII 14-5
expressing regret   IX 31, 44-5
expressing the speaker's
  emotions vividly   VIII 30-1
expressions accompanying
  an action   VII 130-1

169

expressions ending in . . . -nna
    VII 8-9
expressions ending in . . . -yuu
    VII 8-9
expressions for accepting
    an offer   VII 16-7
expressions for idling away
    one's time   VIII 62-3
expressions for reporting   VII 58-9
expressions indicating the cause
    of emotion   X 128-9
expressions indicating the start
    of an action   X 98-9
expressions indicating
    the subject   VI 152-3
expressions meaning "as you
    know"   VI 40-1
expressions meaning "be filled
    with"   X 70-1
expressions meaning "but" X 46-7
expressions meaning "enjoy"
    VIII 114-5
expressions meaning
    "everything"   X 36-7
expressions meaning "I think
    that . . . "   X 116-7
expressions meaning "Isn't
    it . . . ?"   X 38-9
expressions meaning "Just as
    it is now"   VIII 18-9
expressions meaning "keep
    . . . ing"   X 100-1
expressions meaning "must"
    VII 126-7
expressions meaning "not all . . ."
    VI 114-5
expressions meaning "only"
    X 106-7
expressions meaning "please
    accept it"   VI 30
expressions meaning "should
    have"   X 80-1
expressions meaning "to me,
    for me"   X 150-1
expressions meaning "why"
    X 28-9
expressions of apology or grati-
    tude about previous meetings
    VI 12-3
expressions of concern   VII 135
expressions of gratitude   VII 70-1
expressions of gratitude and
    compliments   VI 11
expressions of pain   X 130-1
expressions of pleasure   VI 90-1
expressions used at the end of
    business discussions   VI 18-9
expressions used for admiration
    X 18-9
expressions used for praise X 94-5

expressions used for strong
    denial   VI 116-7
expressions used when offering
    a gift   VIII 22-3
expressions used when starting
    a statement   VI 126-7

F

family language   VI 97
"finish. . . .-ing," expressions
    meaning   VIII 134-5
first part of a sentence
    implying the rest   VI 132-3
fuben   IX 132
-*fune* (counter)   IX 16
futoi   IX 136-7
fuyukai   IX 62

G

"*g*" sound nazalized   VII 115
. . . *ga* (*desu*)   IX 31, 53, 84-5
. . . (*desu*) -*ga*   VI 68-9
(noun, pronoun)-*ga*   VI 153
. . . *ga nai* vs. . . . *ja nai* VIII 82-3
. . . *gachi*   X 62-3
gaman-dekinai   IX 63, 105
gaman-ga tarinai   IX 105
gaman-suru   X 152-3
ganbare   VIII 97
gangan   VI 47
. . . *gari-ya*   X 66-7
. . . *garu*   X 24-5, 66-7, 128-9
genki   VIII 82-3
genki-ja nai vs. *genki-ga nai* VIII 82-3
giving directions   VI 56-7
giving one's card to someone
    VIII 112-3
giving one's name   IX 18-9
giving someone's name without
    any terms of respect   VI 29
giving uncertain information
    VIII 12-3
go + adjectives   VIII 43
go + noun/stem of verb   IX 26-7
gobusata   VIII 51
Gochisoosama (-deshita).   X 14-5
gojibun   VII 148
Gokigen-yoo.   VI 15
Gokuroosama.   VI 63/X 14-5
gomen   X 68-9
Gomen-kudasai(-mase).
    VI 15, 19/X 69
Gomen-nasai.   IX 81/X 68-9
goran-ni naru   VI 120-1
gorogoro (-shite-iru) VII 65/VIII 62-3
gorori-to, goro-t-to   VII 65
gozaimasen sounding like
    gozaasen   VII 114

gozonji (vs. zonjiru)   IX 148-9
Gozonji-desu-ka.   VI 40
gratitude about previous
   meetings   VI 12-3
gratitude, expressions of   VIII 50-1
gratitude for help   VI 38-9
gratitude for someone's help
    VII 38-9
gratitude for someone's kind
   action   VII 38-9
guai   VIII 84
gurai   X 22-3

H

hai implying you want to termi-
   nate the conversation   VII 96-7
hai used to call someone's
   attention to an action   VII 97
hai used to show polite attitude
    VII 88-9
hai, various uses of   VII 96-7
Hai. and Soo-desu.   VII 88-9
Haiken-shimasu.   VIII 149
haiku   VI 154
haitte-iru vs. irete-aru   VI 134-5
hajime-ni   VIII 122-3
hajime-wa   VIII 122-3
hajimete   VIII 122-3
hakkiri shinai   VI 47
hanashikakeru   VI 118-9
hanashikomu   VI 123
hanashite   X 142-3
hantai   IX 51
hara-ga tatsu   IX 62
harau   X 90-1
"Have a good . . ."   VIII 114-5
hazu   VII 68-9
. . . hazu-ga nai   VI 116/VIII 78
hazukashigariya   X 66-7
headache, description of   VI 46-7
hidden sentence subjects   VII 100-5
higamu   VI 111
-hiki (counter)   VIII 74-5
hirihiri   VI 49
hito   VII 149
hito-kuchi   VII 53
hito-yasumi   VII 53
hitori-de   VII 149
hitotsu   VII 53/X 145
. . . hodo   X 8-9, 22-3
. . . hodo-ja nai   X 22-3
-hon (counter)
    VI 128-9/VIII 74/IX 16-7
Honno kimochi-desu.   VI 50-1
honno   VI 50-1/X 107
honto-ni   VIII 36, 60/IX 77
hoomon-suru   IX 125
hosoi   IX 137
hotondo . . . nai   X 87

hotondo   X 21, 86-7
humble speech   VIII 148-9
hyotto suru-to   VI 94

I

"i" dropped in . . . ni naru   VII 83
"i" dropped in . . . te-iru   VII 82
"i" dropped in iku, itta   VII 82
"i" dropped in irassharu   VII 83
"I would like you to"   VIII 108-9
Ichi-ni-no san!   VII 130
ichido   VII 52-3/X 144-5
ichigai-niwa ienai   IX 59
identifying oneself with one's
   family members   VIII 35
. . . (de) ii   IX 112-3
ii kagen   VIII 84-5
ii tokoro   VI 100-1/VII 78
ii-yo   VIII 27
Ii?   VIII 155
Iie, kekkoo-desu.   VI 36
Iie, koko-de shitsuree-shimasu.   VI 24
Iie, sonna koto-wa arimasen.   VIII 106
. . . (to) iimasu   IX 18-9
. . . ijoo (meaning "now that")
    VIII 80-1, IX 8-9
ikaga   IX 51
ikahodo   X 8
(. . . nakereba) ikemasen
    VII 98-9, 126-7
iken   IX 50
ikimashita vs. kimashita   VII 117
ikimasu vs. ikimashoo   VII 74
ikimasu-ka vs. ikimasen-ka   VII 22-3
ikiru   VII 50-1
ikkai   X 144-5
iku   IX 114-5
iku toki vs. itta toki   VI 75
iku-yo vs. iku-wayo   VII 95
ima   X 110-1
ima-doki (vs. kono-goro)   VIII 88-9
ima hitotsu   X 110-1
ima ichi   X 111
imasara   VIII 78-9
imasara-no yoo-ni   VIII 79
imperative form   IX 80-1, 154
imperative in indirect speech
    VII 92-3
implying the sentence is going
   to be negative   VIII 13
implying "too much"   VIII 130-1
indicating a reason   IX 10-1, 14-5
indicating certainty about what
   will happen in the future   VIII 14
indicating subject matter
    IX 110-1, 116-7
indirect development of a
   conversation   VII 100-1

171

indirect expressions
    VI 146-7/X 50-1
indirect requests VII 100-1
inochi IX 134-5
inquiring about someone's
    wishes VIII 20-1
intransitive verbs X 72-3
introducing a relative or
    colleague VIII 72-3
introductory words with -ka
    VII 20-1
inviting conversation IX 100-1
ippai VII 53
iru VIII 116-7
itai vs. iitai VII 112
itsuka VII 20-1
Itte-mairimasu. VI 16-7
Itte-rasshai. VI 16-7

J

Ja. VI 14,19,63/IX 39/X 85
. . . ja (contraction) VII 34-5
. . . ja arimasen-ka VIII 126-7/X 38-9
. . . ja nai (vs. . . . ga nai) VIII 82-3
. . . ja nai-ka-to omoimasu VII 132
Ja, ato-de. VI 16
Ja, ii-na. VIII 66-7
Ja, kore-de shitsuree-shimasu. VI 17
Ja, mata. VI 14, 63/IX 39
Ja, sonna tokoro-de. VI 18
jama (vs. ojama) IX 152-3
. . . jatta VII 34
jibun VII 148-9
jibun-de VII 149
jikan X 127
jinsee IX 134-5
Jitsu-wa . . . VI 20-1
jogen IX 96-7
(o) joozu IX 72-3
juu (vs. chuu) X 54-5
juubun IX 112-3

K

. . . ka dooka X 120
ka in Soo-desu-ka VI 142-3
ka used to show reserve VI 148-9
. . . ka(na) VII 144-5
. . . ka, pronunciation of VIII 92-3
. . . ka-to omoimashite VII 56-7
. . . ka-to omotte . . . X 120-1
kaeroo-tto VII 144-5
kaeru toki vs. kaetta toki VI 74-5
kagen VIII 84-5
kagi vs. kani VII 115
kagiru vs. kagiranai IX 34-5
kai X 144-5
kaite X 142-3
(tema ga) kakaru X 126

kakatte-iru vs. kakerarete-iru X 72-3
kakegoe VII 130
. . . kakeru VI 119
kami-o ichimai vs. ichimai-no
    kami IX 138-9
. . . kamo shirenai VI 94/IX 104
. . . kana VIII 67/IX 138-9
kanai vs. tsuma VI 28
. . . kaneru IX 84
Kangaete-mimasu. IX 94-5
kanji compounds VI 67
kankee X 30-1
kankeesha X 31
kankoku IX 96
(. . . ni) kansuru X 148-9
. . . kara (because)
    VI 26-7/VII 13, 73/IX 11, 14-5, 20-1,
    32-3, 79, 92-3, 100-1/X34-5, 112-3
. . . kara (from) IX 121/X118-9
. . . kara . . .te-kudasai IX 14-5
kashikomarimashita VIII 27
. . . kashira VII 125/IX 118-9
. . . kedo
    IX 20-1, 31, 53, 79, 93, 100-1, 129
kekkoo, uses of X 102-3
kekkoo-desu VIII 119, 153, 155
. . . (de) kekkoo-desu IX 112-3
kenkoo VIII 83
keredomo VI 68-9
. . . kerya VII 35
. . . ki-ga suru X 125
kikite X 142-3
kinben VIII 83
(. . . no) kinjo IX 122-3
-kire (counter) IX 16
kiree X 18-9
. . . kirenai VI 115/VIII 130-1
kirikiri VI 44, 46
. . . kiru VIII 134-5
kitto VIII 14
. . . kko nai VI 116-7
-ko (counter) IX 16-7
kochira VI 108/X 154-5
Kochira . . . desu. VI 8
Kochira-koso. VI 8/VII 150-1
Kochira-koso totsuzen ojama-
    shimashite. VI 25
kogarana IX 127
kogata(-no) IX 127
koitsu X 11
koko vs. kookoo VII 112
koko-n toko VII 86-7
kokoro-bakari-no VIII 48
komakai IX 127
komaru IX 104
komaru/komarimasu used in a
    reprimand VII 90-1
komatte-iru/imasu VII 91
. . . komu VI 122-3
Konbanwa. X 48

172

konna	VII 8-9
Konnichiwa.	X 48
kono	VI 150-1
kono-goro (vs. ima-doki)	VIII 88-9
kono mama	VIII 18-9
koo	X 140-1
koo-yuu	VII 8-9
koofuku (vs. ureshii)	X 40-1
kore vs. kore-wa	VIII 86-7
kore-kara . . . tokoro	VII 78
kore	VI 150-1
kore-wa	X 42-3
Kore-wa kore-wa.	X 42
korobu	VI 48
korya	VI 68/X43
koso	VII 150-1
kotchi	X 155
koto used to mean "necessity"	VI 98-9
. . . (suru) koto-desu	VIII 64-5
. . . koto-ga dekinai	IX 82-3, 84
. . . koto-ni suru	VIII 38
koto-ni yoru-to	VI 94
. . . koto-wa . . . desu-ga	VII 30-1
kotowaru	X 104-5
kotowatte-oku	X 104-5
kotozuke	VI 32
. . . ku	IX 130-1
. . . ku arimasen-ka	X 38-9
. . . ku naru (vs. . . . ni naru)	VII 54/IX 150-1
. . . ku nasasoo	VII 29
. . . kucha	VII 98
kudasai	IX 26-7
kudasaru	VI 53
kurasu	VII 50-1
kure	VII 72
kureru	VI 53
kuru	IX 114-5
kuru hito vs. kita hito	VI 75
kurushii	X 130-1
. . . kya	VII 35, 99
-kyaku (counter)	IX 16
kyooshuku-desu	VIII 107

L

last part of a sentence can be understood	X 135
leaving a message	VI 32-3
leaving out a verb phrase	VII 48-9
leaving out particles	IX 107, 120-1
leaving out the last part	VII 56-7, 66-7
length of sentences	VII 18-9
listener anticipating what will come next	VI 133
listener participating in com-	

pleting the speaker's sentence	VI 137
long vowels, pronunciation of	VII 112-3
looking for the right expression	VIII 110-1

M

"m" sound	VII 114
. . . (de) ma-ni au	IX 113
mada	VIII 140/X 107
mada . . . te-inai	VI 70-1
. . . made	IX 121/X 78-9
magatte vs. mawatte	VII 115
-mai (counter)	VIII 75
Maido arigatoo-gozaimasu.	VI 62
maido	VIII 46-7
making a question sound less demanding	VIII 8-9
making a request	VI 26-7/VIII 24-5, 150-1/IX 14-5, 26-7
making explanations	VI 40-1
making sure that the other person finds it convenient to talk on the phone	VIII 155
making verbs from adjectives	X 24-5
Makoto-ni tsumarai mono-desu-ga.	VI 30
makoto-ni	VIII 22
male speech used toward women	VII 124-5
. . . (ta) mama	VIII 18-9/IX 37
marude	IX 77
. . . mase	VI 120
. . . masen-ka	IX 65
mashi	VII 40-1/IX 24-5
. . . mashita	VI 70
. . . mashite	VI 81
. . . mashoo-ka	VIII 20-1, 109
. . . masu	VII 74-5
. . . masu vs. . . . te-kudasai used for giving directions	VI 56-7
mattaku	VIII 36
. . . me	IX 146-7
meals, words referring to	VIII 56-7
-mee (-sama)	VIII 28-9
meeshi	VI 9
meeshi-o doozo	VIII 113
men's & women's sentence endings in familiar conver-sation	VII 94-5
meshi vs. ohiru	VII 124-5
mi-ni iku	IX 125
mimetic words	VII 64-5
mimicry words	VI 140-1
minna	X 36-7
minshuku	VI 62/VIII 84
mitsukaru vs. mitsukeru	VII 60-1

173

. . . mo (vs. . . . wa) X 114-5
. . . mo aru-shi, . . . mo aru X 108-9
mochi-yoru X 147
mochiron VI 144-5
. . . mon (o) X 74-5
mon(o)-(desu-)ka VI 116
mono meaning "should" VII 68-9
moo . . . kirenai VIII 131
Moo ichido iimashoo-ka. IX 55
moo sugu VIII 140
moo sukoshi-de . . . suru tokoro-
datta VI 101
moo sukoshi-de X 87
Moo takusan-desu. VIII 118-9
moo, uses of VIII 140-1
Mooshiagemasu. VIII 149
. . . (to) mooshimasu. IX 18-9
Mooshiwake arimasen.
VII 17, 72-3/IX 109
mooshiwake nai-n-desu-ga . . .
VIII 103/IX 22
moshika-shitara VI 94-5
moshika-suru-to VI 94-5
moshimoshi VII 11/VIII 98-9
motte-kitageru VII 34
must, expressions meaning
VII 126-7
musuko-san X 58

N

. . . n ja nai-deshoo-ka VII 132
. . . n(o)-desu-ne IX 56
. . . n(o)de IX 32-3
. . . n-da-kara IX 92-31/X 136-7
. . . n-da-kedo IX 92-3
. . . n-dane IX 56
. . . n-desu X 136-7
. . . (na) n-desu-ga . . . VIII 24-5
. . . n-desu-ka (vs. . . . desu-ka)
IX 64-5
. . . n-desu-kedo VII 13
. . . n-ja arimasen VI 138-9
. . . (na) n-ja nai-deshoo-ka VIII 10-1
. . . n-ja nai-ka-to omoimasu VI 149
. . . (suru) n-nara VIII 70-1
(dictionary form +) na IX 154-5
. . . na (negative imperative)
VI 82-3/VII 93
. . . na (used as familiar confirmation) VIII 66-7
. . . na (used for a familiar
command) VI 84-5
. . . na (used when talking to
oneself) VIII 30-1, 66
. . . na to omou VIII 30
nado VII 120-1/X 51
nado-to yuu mono/koto/no VII 120-1
nagaiki VII 50-1

. . . nagara IX 30-1
. . . nai . . . wa nai
VIII 146-7/IX 128-9
. . . nai-ka-to omoimashite . . .
(polite requests) VII 56-7
. . . nai-ka-to omotte . . . X 120-1
. . . nai-no IX 155
. . . nai-to komarimasu VII 90-1
. . . naide(-kudasai/-ne) IX 142, 154
. . . naide sumu VII 14-5
nakanaka VIII 10-1, 126
. . . nakereba VII 90-1, 99, 126
. . . nakereba komarimasu
VII 90-1, 99
. . . nakereba narimasen VII 99, 126
. . . nakereba yokatta X 81
. . . nakerya VII 126
. . . nakucha (dame-desu)
VII 98-9, 126-7
nakusu IX 88
. . . nakute IX 143
. . . nakute-wa narimasen/
ikemasen VII 98, 126
. . . nakya VII 98-9, 126-7
name card VI 9
nan-datte X 28-9
nan-nara/-deshitara IX 144-5
nan-to naku X 12, 125
nandaka VIII 82/X 124-5
nande X 28
nandemo VII 42-3/VIII 12-3
Nandemo . . . soo-desu. VIII 12-3
nani-kara nani-made VIII 33/X 36-7
Nani-o sashiagemashoo-ka. VIII 21
nanika VII 20-1
nanishiro (vs. tonikaku) X 122-3
. . . nanka VI 153
. . . nante VII 120-1
nantoka X 12-3
nantoka . . . dekiru VI 37
naosu vs. naoru IX 70-1
narimasen VII 126-7
narimasen left out VII 98-9
naru VII 54-5
. . . nasai VI 84, 120-1/IX 80-1
. . . nashi-de IX 142-3
nazalized "g" sound VII 115
naze X 28
. . . ne VIII 30, 66-7/IX 46-7
. . . ne (added to phrases)
VII 26-7, 152-3
. . . ne, intonation of VI 143, IX 46-7
nee VII 10-1
. . . negaimasu IX 26-7
negation of a reason VI 138-9
negative attitude X 101
negative form in questions VII 22-3
negative forms of . . . soo-desu
VII 28-9

174

negative imperatives
                              VI 82/IX 154-5
. . . ni (left out)   IX 120-1, 124-5
. . . ni (used for connecting
    nouns or pronouns)   X 44-5
. . . ni (vs. . . . de)   VIII 116-7
. . . ni (vs. . . . e)   VIII 138-9
. . . ni (vs. . . . kara)   X 118-9
. . . ni (vs. . . . tame-ni) IX 114-5
. . . ni chigainai   IX 104
. . . ni iku/kuru   IX 124-5
. . . ni kansuru   X 148-9
. . . ni naru (vs. . . . ku naru)
                             VII 54-51/IX 150-1
. . . ni naru (vs. . . . suru)   X 60
. . . ni naru (vs. . . . . yoo-ni naru)
                             IX 102-3
. . . ni . . . ni   X 44-5
. . . ni oite   X 148-9
. . . ni suginai   X 106-7
. . . ni taishite   X 64-5, 148-9
. . . ni totte   X 64-5, 148-9
. . . ni tsuite   X 82-3
. . . ni yotte   X 148-9
. . . ni yotte (chiagau)   IX 58-9
ni-san   VIII 91
nihon-no (two)   VI 128-9
nikoniko, niko-t-to   VII 65
. . . nikui   VII 84-5
-nin (counter)   VIII 75
. . . niwa osewa-ni natte-orimasu
                             VI 10
no (thing)   X 11
. . . no hoo-ga   IX 24-5
. . . no koto   VII 155/X 82-3
. . . no koto(-o) vs. . . . ni tsuite
                             VIII 132-3
. . . no koto-desu   VII 154-5
. . . no koto-desu-ga   VI 126-7
. . . no mae-ni   X 149
. . . no mae-no   X 149
. . . no mama   IX 37
no often becoming n   VII 86
no-desu becoming n-desu   VII 56-7
nochi-hodo   X 9
. . . node
    VI 26-7/VII 13/IX 11, 79, 84-5/X 34-5
. . . node vs. . . . n-da-kara   X 136-7
nomimasen vs. nomemasen   IX 75
. . . nomo shikata-ga nai   VII 139
nonbiri-suru   VI 93
. . . none   IX 56-7
. . . noni vs. . . . keredomo   VI 76-7
. . . noni   VI 76-7
"not all . . ."   VI 114-5
not introducing someone
    present by his name   VIII 72-3
noun + desu   VII 136-7
. . . nowa   VII 121
number of syllables   VI 154-5

o
. . . o   IX 106-7, 120-1/X 128-9
o- (added to adjectives)   VIII 42-3
. . . o + number + verb   IX 138-9
o . . . (ita) shimashoo   X 32
O . . . deshita-ka   VI 124-5
O . . . deshoo-ka   VI 125
O . . . desu-ka
    VI 124-5/VII 134-5/VIII 144-5
                             148-9/X96-7
(O) . . . nasaimasu-ka   X 96
o often dropping   VII 87
O . . . kudasai.
                VIII 144-5, 148-9/IX 26-7
O . . . shimasu.   VIII 148-9
o. . . .ni naru   VII 134-5/IX 66-7
obasan vs. obaasan   VII 113
Ocha-mo sashiagemasen-de.   VI 25
odekake-desu-ka   VII 135
offering & receiving a gift VIII 48
offering to do a favor   X 32-3
Ohayoo-gozaimasu.   X 48-9
oi   VII 11
oisogashii tokoro   VII 79
ojama vs. jama   IX 152-3
Ojikan-o torimashite.   VI 19
ojisan vs. ojiisan   VII 112
okaeri-desu-ka   VII 134-5
Okaeri-nasai.   VI 120/IX 81
okage   VI 43
Okagesama-de.   VI 39
Okaimono-desu-ka.   X 96-7
okane-ga nakute   VII 12-3
Oki-o tsukete.   IX 38-9
okoru   IX 62-3
okusan   VII 129/X 58-9
okyakusama-atsukai   X 26
okyakusan   VII 129
Ome-ni kakarimasu.   VIII 149
Omochi-shimashoo-ka.   VIII 20
omoidasanai vs. omoidasenai IX 74-5
omoshirokunai   IX 62
omou   X 116-7
onajimi   VIII 46-7
Onegai-(ita)shimasu.
        VI 23, 38/VII 16-7/VIII 101/IX 108
onegai-da-kara   VII 46-7
onna vs. onna-no-hito   VI 132
onomatopoeic words   VI 140-1
oo vs. oooo   VII 113
. . . (y) oo-to omoimasu   VII 24-5
. . . (y) oo-tto   VII 144-5
ookii vs. ookina   X 56-7
opening a conversation   VII 118-9
orusu-ni   VI 34
Osaki-ni (shitsuree-shimasu). X 14-5
osameru   X 90-1
osawagase-suru   VIII 46-7

oseji (vs. compliment) VIII 106-7
Osewa-ni narimashita. VIII 69
Osewasama (-deshita). VI 63/X 14-5
oshiete-itadaku VIII 58-9
oshiete-kudasai IX 97
oshikomu VI 122-3
osoku natte VII 12-3
Osoreirimasu. VI 38/VII 17/VIII 107
Osoreirimasu-ga/ kedo . . .
VIII 144, 151
Otaku-kara denwa-desu. VI 29
otesuu VIII 51
otesuu-desu-ga VII 17
otoko vs. *otoko-no-hito* VI 132
otoosan VII 129
otosu IX 88
Otsukaresama. VI 14, 62-3
. . . owaru VIII 134-5
Oyasumi-nasai. VI 120/IX 81/X48
oyobitate VI 19

P

paper-recycling truck announcement VIII 46-7
particles at the end of sentences
(*ne, yo, wayo*) VIII 30-1
particles meaning "in/at, etc."
VIII 116-7
particles meaning "to" VIII 138-9
passive form VI 54
phonetic changes in rapid speech
VII 82-3, 86-7, 98-9
phrases ending with . . .*te* VII 12-3
phrases with *ne* VII 152-3
physical distance between the
speakers VI 8
pika-t-to VII 64-5
pikapika VII 64-5
pikari(-to) VII 64-5
pittari VI 140-1
plain imperative VI 82/VI 92-3
"please accept it" VI 30
pleasure, expressions of VI 90-1
polite expression of opposition
VII 132-3
polite questions VIII 52-3
polite refusal VIII 48-9, 152-3
polite requests VII 56-7
politely asking about someone's
opinion or wishes VIII 8-9
position of phrases indicating
numbers VI 129
potential form IX 82, 102-3
. . . ppanashi IX 36-7
. . . ppoi VI 110-1
praising one's family VII 40-1
praising someone's skill IX 72-3
preliminary remarks
VI 126-7/VII 41

process of receiving a gift VI 30-1
pronunciation making the meaning clear VI 107
pronunciation of certain
sentence particles VIII 92-3
pun VI 155
pun between *kaeru* & *kaeru* VII 145

Q

questions, polite VIII 52-3
quotation VII 93

R

ra, re becoming *n* VII 35
redundancy VI 60-1
referring to consecutive actions
IX 12-3
referring to losing things,
expressions IX 88-9
refusal to an offer
VI 31, 36/VIII 48-9, 152
repeated expression of gratitude
or apology VI 13
repeating similar expressions
VI 19
replying to praise VIII 106-7
reporting something bad VIII 69
reserved endings VII 132-3
responding to a compliment
VI 42-3/VII 30-1, 40
responding to invitation-like
comments VIII 60-1
response, frequent (*aizuchi*)
VIII 98-9
rhetorical question VI 116-7
rippana X 94-5

S

sagatte vs. *sawatte* VII 115
saki-hodo X 9
sakihodo-wa VI 13
-sama VIII 28-9
Samui-desu-ka. vs. *Samui-n-
desu-ka.* IX 64-5
sansee IX 51
sappari, uses of VIII 120-1
sarcasm, expression of VII 141
. . . sareru VI 66-7/VII 92/X 61
. . . saseru vs. *. . . . te-morau*
VIII 40-1
satto VI 140-1
sawagaseru VIII 46-7
saying goodbye (in a telephone
conversation) VIII 102-3
sayonara VI 14-5, 16, 19
seekatsu IX 134-5
seemee IX 134-5

Seeno!   VII 130
sekkaku . . . noni   VI 77
sekkaku-desu-kara   VIII 48
self-defense   VI 96
semai   IX 126-7
Senjitsu-wa gochisoosama-
  deshita.   VI 12
sensee   X 17
sentence endings in familiar
  conversation   VII 94-5
sentence particles, pronun-
  ciation of   VIII 92-3
sentence subject   VI 152-3
Setsumee-shite-kudasai.   IX 52
sharply inhaling or sucking
  teeth during speech   VI 131
. . . shi   VII 66-7/X 108-9
shika   IX 29
shikashi   X 46
shikata-ga nai/arimasen   VII 138-9
shikushiku   VI 44
Shitsuree-desu-ga . . .
                           VIII 150-1/IX 22
Shitsuree-shimasu.   VI 15, 19
Shitte-imasu-ka.   VI 40
(o) shokuji   VIII 56-7
shoochi-shimashita   VIII 27
short and long vowels   VII 112-3
showing the speaker's reserve
  in expressing his opinion
                                  VIII 10-1
shujin vs. shuujin   VII 112
signals to show that one is
  going to start talking   VI 130
signals to show the start of
  business discussions   VI 20
signs and written instructions
                                     VI 83
silence to show hesitation   VII 133
"small," expressions meaning
                                 IX 126-7
(. . . no) soba   IX 122-3
sochira   VI 108-9/X 155
soitsu   X 11
soko vs. sooko   VII 113
soko-de   VII 63
something that the speaker
  cannot control   VI 72-3
Sonna koto(-wa) arimasen(-yo).
                             VIII 106, 125
sonna   VI 117/VII 8-9/VIII 79
sono vs. ano   VI 150-1
. . . soo ja nai/arimasen   VII 28-9
Soo omoimasu.   X 140-1
Soo-deshoo-ka.   VII 132-3/VIII 9
Soo-desu.   VII 88-9
. . . soo-desu (appearance)
                        VII 28-9, 42/X25, 66
. . . soo-desu (message)
                         VI 34-5/VII 58-9

Soo-desu-ka, intonation of   VI 142-3
. . . soo-mo nai/arimasen
                            VII 28-9/IX 85
soo-yuu   VII 8-9
soo-yuu koto-de   VI 18
soodan-suru vs. oshiete-itadaku
                                 VIII 58-9
sore   VI 150-1
sore-dake   IX 28-9
sore-de   VI 136-7/VII 63
Sore-ja, yoroshiku.   VI 18
sore-mo soo-desu-ga   VIII 37
sore-wa soo-desu-ne   VIII 36-7
sore-wa   VI 68/VII 36-7
sorosoro   VIII 34
sorya/soryaa . . .   VI 68-9
sotchi   X 155
sounding hesitant or apologetic
  when making a request   VI 27
sounds difficult to hear   VII 112-7
speaker and listener partici-
  pating in a flow of speech   VI 81
speaker's attitude   VI 134-5
speaker's will   VI 72-3
starting a statement   VI 126-7
stem + -wa shinai   VI 106-7
stomachache, description of
                                   VI 44-5
subarashii   IX 73/X 18
subjects determined only by
  the situation   VII 105
subjects indicated by the use
  of humble expression   VII 103
subjects indicated by the use
  of polite terms   VII 102-3
subjects obvious from the
  situation   VII 104-5
suffering from someone's
  actions   VI 54-5
suggestion, making a   VII 52-3
Sumimasen.   VII 14, 72-3/IX 109
Sumimasen-deshita.   VI 39
Sumimasen-ga/kedo . . .   VIII 151
sumu (live)   VII 50-1/VIII 116-7
sumu (suffice)   VII 14-5
surimuku   VI 49
. . . suru (used to mean
  "to cost")   VI 92-3
. . . suru (vs. . . . ni naru)   X 60-1
. . . suru koto-ga aru   VI 98-9
. . . suru koto-ni naru   VI 98-9
. . . suru koto-ni suru   VI 98-9
. . . suru-to komaru/komarimasu
                                   VII 91
susumeru   IX 97
suteki   X 18-9
sutto   VI 140-1
suu-   VIII 90-1
sympathy, an expression of
                                 VIII 69

T

. . . ta ato-de (vs. . . . te-kara) X 88-9
. . . ta bakari   VI 47/VII 146-7
ta form   VI 38-9
. . . ta hoo-ga ii   VII 24-5/VIII 54-5, 65
. . . ta ijoo   IX 8-9
. . . ta koto-ga aru   VI 98-9
. . . ta tokoro   VI 101/VII 79, 146-7
. . . ta tokoro-de   VI 101
ta used to indicate the
    completion of an action   VI 74-5
tabena vs. taberu-na   VI 84
tabun   VI 94-5
. . . tagaru   VII 35/X 25
-tai (counter)   VIII 75
taihen (very)   IX 77
taihen, uses of   VIII 68-9
Taihen-desu-ne.   VII 48-9/VIII 68-9
Taihen shitsuree-itashimashita.
    VIII 103
taishita   VI 37
takusan, uses of   VIII 118-9
talking to oneself   VII 25, 144
. . . tame-ni (vs. . . . ni)   IX 114-5
tanka   VI 154
tanomu   VII 17
tanomu-kara   VII 46-7
tanoshii   VIII 114-5
tanoshimu   VIII 114-5
taoreru   VI 48
. . . tara (and found that)
    VII 79, 80-1/IX 12-3
. . . tara (condition)
    VIII 70-1/IX 60-1/X 84
. . . (t)tara (subject)
    VII 153/IX 86-7, 100-1
. . . tara doo-desu-ka   VIII 55
. . . tara ikaga-desu-ka   VIII 55
. . . (t)tara nai   IX 87
. . . tari   X 109
Tasukarimashita.   VI 19, 39
Tasukarimasu.   VII 17
tazunete-iku   IX 125
tazunete-kuru   VI 52-3/IX 125
-te, meaning "a person who . . . "
    X 142-3
te form
    VI 72-3, 80-1/IX 10-1, 12-3, 46-7,
    78-9/X 112-3
te form of adjectives   IX 130-1
te form, pronouncing   IX 90-1
. . . te iku/kaeru   X 79
. . . te used to end a sentence
    VI 80-1
. . . te used to indicate a reason
    VI 72-3/IX 10-1
. . . te used with expressions
    of apology and gratitude
    VIII 50-1

. . . te-ageru   IX 71/X 32
. . . te-aru (with transitive verbs)
    X 73
. . . te-hoshii   VIII 108-9
. . . te-iku   VII 55
. . . te-imasen vs. . . . masen-
    deshita   VI 70-1
. . . te-irassharu   VIII 43, 44-5
. . . te-iru tokoro   VI 101/VII 78
. . . te-iru vs. . . . te-aru   VI 134-5
. . . te-itadaite . . .   VII 70-1
. . . te-itadakenai-deshoo-ka   IX 119
. . . te-itadaku   VI 104-5
. . . te-kara (vs. . . . ta ato-de)
    X 88-9
. . . te-kudasai   IX 14-5, 26, 46, 154
. . . te-kudasaru   VII 38/X 151
. . . te-kudasatte . . .   VII 71
. . . te-kureru   VI 53/VII 38-9/X 151
. . . te-kurete . . .   VII 71
. . . te-kuru
    VI 52-3, 113/VII 55/X 98-9, 150-1
. . . te-miru   IX 94-5
. . . te-miru vs. . . . (y)oo-to
suru   VII 81
. . . te-miru-to   VII 80-1
. . . te-mitara   VII 80-1/IX 12-3
. . . te-moraenai-kana vs.
    . . . te-moraenai?   IX 118-9
. . . te-moraitai   VIII 20-1, 109
. . . te-moratte . . .   VII 71
. . . te-ne   VI 80-1, 85/IX 46-7, 100-1
. . . te-oku   VI 135
. . . te-shimau
    VII 32-3/VIII 129/IX 44-5
. . . te-wa ikemasen   VI 83, 87
. . . te-wa komarimasu   VI 87/VII 91
. . . te-wa used to emphasize
    contrast between two phrases
    VII 44-5
. . . te-wa used to indicate
    condition   VI 86-7
. . . te-yo   IX 46-7
telephone conversation
    VIII 94-5, 98-9, 102-3
tema   X 126-7
tema-doru   X 126-7
tesuu   X 127
thanking in advance   IX 108-9
thanking someone for his
    kindness to one's family
    member   VI 11
thinking in kanji   VI 65
. . . to (and)   X 44, 132
(color) to (color)   IX 151
. . . to (vs. . . . eba, tara)   IX 60
. . . to (vs. . . . to issho-ni)   IX 42-3
. . . to (vs. . . . toka)   VIII 76-7
"to become . . .," expressions
    meaning   IX 102-3

. . . (suru) to ii VIII 54-5
. . . to iimashite-mo VII 77
. . . to iimasu/mooshimasu IX 18-9
. . . to ittatte VII 77
. . . to itte-imasu X 25, 66
. . . to itte-mo VII 76-7
. . . to kitara IX 110-1
. . . to mooshimashite-mo VII 77
. . . to omoimashite VII 56-7
. . . to omoimasu VIII 10-1/X116-7, 140-1
. . . to omotte VII 56-7
. . . to omou X 116-7
. . . to osshaimashita VI 35
"to visit," expressions meaning IX 124-5
. . . to yuu hanashi-desu VII 43
. . . to yuu koto-desu VII 43, 59
. . . to yuu koto-ni narimasu-ne IX 57
. . . to yuu wake-desu VII 122
. . . toita VII 35
toka VIII 76-7/X 44-5, 50-1, 132-3
tokoro contracted to toko VII 86-7
. . . tokoro made-wa ikanai VI 115
tokoro VI 100-1/VII 78-9/IX 122-3
toku vs. tooku VII 113
tomaru VIII 116-7
tomo VI 144-5
tondemo nai (vs. iie) VII 104-5
tone and the speaker's intention VI 69
tonikaku X 122-3
-too (counter) VIII 74
. . . (no) toori IX 40-1, 140-1
torareru X 90-1
(tema o) toru X 126
toshi VIII 124-5
toshi-ni niawazu VIII 125
totemo IX 76-7
totemo totemo IX 76
Totsuzen ojama-itashimashite. VI 25
. . . towa kagiranai IX 34
transitive & intransitive verbs VII 60-1/IX 70-1
tsugoo IX 132-3
tsui (. . . te-shimau) VIII 128-9
tsukareru IX 104-5
tsukiai-kirenai VIII 131
tsuma VI 28
tsumaranai mono-desu-ga/ mon(o)-da-kedo VIII 22-3, 48
tsumori VII 75/IX 66-7
tsurai X 130-1
tsure VI 22
tsutomeru VIII 116-7
-tsuu (counter) VIII 75
tsuujiru IX 113
. . . tsuzukeru X 100-1
. . . tte (conveying a message) VI 35, 82-3/VII 59, 100-1

. . . tte (indicating subject matter) VI 152-3/IX 100-1
. . . tto VII 144-5

U

"u" in masu, desu devocalized VII 116-7
uchi-kara X 151
ukagau VIII 60-1, 149, 152
ukkari-suru VIII 129
umai IX 72-3
unexpected development in conversation VII 37
unnecessary subject in the second sentence VII 37
ureshii VI 90-1/X 40-1
urite X 142-3
use of pronouns X 155
use of the negative form in questions VII 114-5
ushinau IX 89
using greater number of steps VI 127
using ne between phrases VII 26-7
usui IX 136-7

V

verbal politeness VI 104-5,127
verbs often left out VII 136-7
visiting someone without notice VI 24
voiceless vowels VII 116-7
vowels, length of VII 112-3

W

. . . wa (at the end of a sentence) VIII 16-7
. . . wa (indicating subject matter) IX 111,117
. . . wa (used to indicate contrast) VII 44-5, 106-7/VIII 32-3
. . . wa (used to mean "not all . . .") VII 114-5/VIII 32-3
. . . wa (vs. . . . ga) VI 78-9
. . . wa (vs. . . . mo) X 114-5
. . . wa, leaving out VI 153/VIII 86-7
. . . wa? (polite questions) VIII 52-3
-wa (counter) VIII 74/IX 17
. . . wa arigatoo-gozaimashita VII 70-1
. . . wa shitsuree-shimashita VI 13
waka VI 154-5
Wakarimasen. IX 52-3
Wakarimashita. VIII 26-7
Wakarimashita-ka. IX 54
wakatcha VII 44
Wakatta. VIII 27

179

wake VII 122
. . . wake ja arimasen VI 115, 138-9
. . . wake-desu VII 122-3
. . . wane VIII 17, 67
warui tokoro VI 101
Warui(-ne/-wane). VI 38
warui-kedo VII 16-7
warui-n-desu/da-kedo . . . IX 22
Warukatta(-ne/-wane). VI 39
Wasshoi! VII 131
watashi-ga vs. watashi-wa VI 78-9
watashi-ni X 150-1
watashi-wa VII 106-7
. . . wayo VIII 17
wife reporting her husband's
    absence from the office VI 29
words with a negative impli-
    cation X 63

Y

. . . ya (and) VIII 77/X 44-5, 50, 132
. . . ya (sentence particle) X 92-3
yareru IX 113
yarikirenai IX 104-5
yari-kirenai VIII 131
yaru vs. ageru VIII 34-5
yaru vs. suru VIII 38-9
. . . yasui & . . . nikui VII 54-5
yatsu X 10-1
. . . yo VIII 30, 92-3/IX 47
(. . . na)-yo VI 84
Yoisho! VII 130-1
yoji vs. yooji VII 113
yokattara vs. yokereba IX 60-1
yoku X 76-7
yoku, meaning "much"
    X 76-7, 134-5

yoku, various uses of VII 140-1
yoku nai-ne vs. yoku nai-wane VII 95
yonderu VII 34
yonjattara VII 34
. . . yoo IX 140-1
yoo (used to attract someone's
    attention) VII 10-1
. . . yoo(-ga nai) IX 82-3
. . . yoo-desu-ga VII 132
. . . (no) yoo-ni IX 41
. . . yoo-ni naru VII 54-5/IX 102-3
. . . yoo-ni yuu IX 96-7
. . . yoo-to omoimasu VII 24-5
. . . yoo-tto VII 144-5
. . . yori IX 121/X 146-7
. . . yori shikata-ga nai VII 138
yori-kakaru X 147
Yoroshii-deshoo-ka. VIII 154-5/IX 55
yoroshiku VI 90
Yoroshiku doozo. IX 68-9
Yoroshiku onegai-shimasu. IX 108
yoru X 146-7
"you" in Japanese VII 128-9
yoyaku VI 60
yukkuri-suru VI 93

Z

zaazaa VI 141
Zehi oide-kudasai. VIII 14
zehi VIII 14-5, 60-1
zenbu X 36-7
zenbu vs. zenbu-wa VIII 32-3
zenzen IX 77
zonjiru (vs. gozonji) IX 148-9
zuibun VIII 118
zukinzukin VI 46
zukizuki VI 46, 49
zutsuu VI 47